THE SUPPORT-RAISING HANDBOOK

A Guide for Christian Workers

Brian Rust & Barry McLeish

INTERVARSITY PRESS
DOWNERS GROVE, ILLINOIS 60515

InterVarsity Press is the book-publishing division of Inter-Varsity Christian Fellowship, a student movement active on campus at hundreds of universities, colleges and schools of nursing. For information about local and regional activities, write IVCF, 233 Langdon St., Madison, WI 53703.

Distributed in Canada through InterVarsity Press, 860 Denison St., Unit 3, Markham, Ontario L3R 4H1, Canada.

ISBN 0-87784-326-0

Printed in the United States of America

Library of Congress Cataloging in Publication Data

Rust, Brian, 1957-
    The support-raising handbook.

    Bibliography: p.
      1. Church fund raising.   I. McLeish, Barry, 1956-
II. Title.
BV772.5.R87   1984   254.8   84-22448
ISBN 0-87784-326-0

18	17	16	15	14	13	12	11	10	9	8	7	6	5	4	3	2
98	97	96	95	94	93	92	91	90	89	88	87	86	85			

for
Jacque and Deborah

Acknowledgments

In its "dream" stage this book was given substance by Peter Northrup, senior vice president of Inter-Varsity Christian Fellowship. Our sincere thanks to him and to Ron Nicholas, director of marketing, for providing the opportunity and environment to do this book. Also, thanks go to our marketing associates, particularly in the development department: most notably Bill Chickering for his early critical comments, Jimmy Locklear who provided early direction and Carol Grady's staff who were a great help. Perhaps most of all we would like to thank the hundreds of Inter-Varsity staff serving on campuses throughout the country. Their ideas, practices and commitment in support raising lend credibility to this handbook. Finally, the editorial staff at InterVarsity Press helped shape our thoughts and gave the book cohesiveness.

Our thanks to all.

Barry McLeish
Brian Rust

Preface

Sarah, a missionary teacher, wants to raise her support according to scriptural principles, and yet the Bible doesn't address all her questions. Bob and Judy want to get to Taiwan as quickly as possible, but do they have to become professional fundraisers to do so? Henry is having trouble getting enough money for his campus work. Must he make people feel guilty in order to get a response? Many Christian workers have questions about how fundraising fits into their ministry. They serve many people in a variety of roles—as pastors, leaders, speakers, planners, evangelists, technicians, evaluators, counselors, encouragers and fundraisers.

This book addresses that last concern. The principles we use apply to support raising in a variety of settings. We've written this to orient and train Christian workers to gain support for their ministry. We want to present the big picture, and so we begin with some scriptural views on raising support and the roles it has had in the history of Christian missions. From there we present the tools needed to develop a solid support base. We also offer ways to analyze the type and method of communication you want to send and to whom. And finally, we give guidelines for developing a strategy to get the job done.

The principles we give can be used both by those who are new or who have been in ministry for many years. Feel free to copy the forms provided and apply the examples to your own situation.

Raising support is not easy. We know that from experience. It takes prayer, work and time. Our hope is that after reading this book you will see support raising as a ministry that can be done effectively.

1

Support as Ministry

Finally! Louis made his decision to plunge into full-time Christian work. Everything was proceeding according to plan. He had met his supervisor and seen his job description; he knew where he needed to move and had an armful of literature from his agency.

But now he was thinking about what his supervisor told him: "Everyone we accept is required to raise all of his or her budget before reporting. This means approximately $18,000 for a first-year worker. It includes travel, salary, training and administration."

"Eighteen thousand dollars!" Louis thought. "Sounds like a lot of money. But at least I know others have done it. I guess I can too. But where do I start? How long will it take me? I want to get on the job as soon as possible—that's why I joined. But I don't know much about this fundraising business. . . . "

The cost of ministry today—whether counted in time, money or effort—is immense. Unfortunately, the fundraising task isn't always as clearly defined as the mission for which we were hired. Too often this only fuels our anxieties and makes for a bad start in Christian work.

But it doesn't need to be that way. Many Christian workers are successfully raising their support with a bright perspective. Their organizations are helping them with training, a well-defined mission, and a clear and complete plan to pull it all together. Is it easy? No. Is it fun? In some respects—if one considers support raising as ministry. We believe it is.

Funds versus Support

Support raising is not extra or separate from our overall task and calling into Christian service. Most speak of *fund*raising. We emphasize *support* raising. The difference is subtle but real. It concerns how one looks at this task which can either enable or hinder our mission. Fundraising implies money only. It's a quick and dirty term for what some feel is a quick and dirty task.

But asking friends and family to help us is essential to our mission. Without people standing behind us encouraging, giving and praying, we won't be able to help the poor, counsel students or share the gospel in Indonesia. Support more accurately describes what we will need to carry out our mission. And we need more than money; we need partners.

In support raising the emphasis is on relationships with people interested in us or our ministry. It involves an exchange of gifts and abilities between us and our supporters that is pleasing to God. He has blessed us with a call to ministry and them with the resources to help carry it out. How encouraging to realize people care enough about us and our mission to lend support! And how rewarding it will be for them as they obey God by giving and praying to further his gospel through us. Thus we have a ministry to those who send us as well as to those we are sent to.

Personal versus Organizational

Raising support for Christian service can take one of two approaches. The first, personal support, places the emphasis and responsibility on the Christian worker to gather money and prayers. The focus is on him or her as the object of contribution. This is the traditional practice. But while it seems to work well in many situations, personalized support raising is not without its difficulties.

One of these has to do with our philosophy of self. Are people really called to support *me* or the greater mission I'm involved in? What happens when someone decides not to support me? How do I avoid feeling rejected? How do I stop wondering whether or not I said or did the right thing in my supporter's mind? Placing the emphasis on *me* may afford a more personal bond between us, but it may also divert attention from the mission itself.

This leads to the second approach—asking for the gift on behalf of the mission itself. Not, "Will you give to my support?" but rather, "Will you support XYZ's mission, of which I am a part?" On the positive side is the attention one might divert away from self and toward the mission. In some respects this makes it easier to raise and maintain support. If, for example, we didn't know many people who would support us personally, we could rely on those who were interested in our mission agency or field. Parents of students are a prime example for organizations such as Inter-Varsity and Campus Crusade. For most it doesn't matter who *we* are as long as our work is in an area they are concerned about.

This approach also takes a lot of the burden of support raising off the individual missionary. Personal support assumes we are personally responsible. And to some extent that's true. Team or mission support spreads the potential anxiety a little thinner; support raising becomes an easier pill to swallow because we are reducing the risk. As in evangelism, if someone turns us down, they're not really rejecting *us*. They are just not interested in (or can't give toward) the mission.

But reducing the risk sometimes reduces the interdependence Scripture talks about between missionaries and their supporters. Gifts for a mission or team can keep us from communicating appreciation, joys and needs. In an effort to protect ourselves from indebtedness to supporters, we sometimes lose appreciation for their help. We're not as inclined to feel we need to keep in touch, so we don't. Sometimes we even think, "Well, if they're really interested in the mission, they'll keep supporting the work whether they hear from me or not." Removing the personal element from support raising may reduce personal risks, but it will also keep us from developing relationships with those who care about us and our work.

In fact, a combination of personal and mission support-raising perspectives are important. Most of the examples and suggestions in this book deal with personalized support. But different situations will call for different strategies. You are the one who must decide what's best—not only to raise full support, but also to maintain integrity in your support ministry.

We have spoken and worked with many people who have made support ministry a vital and growing part of their overall mission. We've divided the process into four main areas.

1. Knowing your *audiences*—who and where they are, what their interests are, and why they might support you or your work (chapter five).

2. Understanding your position and needs, and combining them into a *case statement* for support (chapters four and six).

3. Identifying and using the *tools for communicating* your mission and need (chapter seven).

4. Drawing together the first three points into a *plan* for raising full support (chapter nine).

This book will explore these elements systematically so you may see how the process develops. Several other points will wind in and about these basics to give you a clear idea of how to proceed.

2

Support Raising and Biblical Models

Biblical perspectives on raising support is a volatile
subject. People disagree about what the correct biblical model is.
A common mistake is to decide on a method and then search for
verses to substantiate the view. And yet, having a solid biblical
foundation on which to base our support-raising practices is
important.

Scripture actually appears to endorse several approaches to
raising support. We will cover them by highlighting scriptural
responses to many commonly asked questions about support
raising.

What Is the Purpose of Property and Money?
In the days of Israel, wealth was often spoken of in terms of land
owned. Tribal bodies gained control of the Promised Land and
segmented it, giving each family their share. The owner of the
land, though, was the Lord (Lev 25:23).

And his people, as outlined in Deuteronomy 14:28-29, had
specific charges as to how the produce of the land was to be
divided, with specific duties assigned to the care of the poor.
Wealth was not a blessing in and of itself. Rather, it could be a
sign of blessing. It seems that it was more often a sign of God's
grace, not of merit.

Everything we have is "on loan" from God. Possessions and property are provided for us to glorify God, to learn and practice good stewardship and to build integrity (1 Chron 29:14-17). The Old Testament also notes that money does not help in times of death or distress (Job 36:19; Ps 52:7). Most importantly, money does not buy God's favor, as Job 34:19 explains.

In the New Testament, perhaps the most popular reference to money is Matthew 6:24: "No one can serve two masters. . . . You cannot serve God and mammon." Jesus seems to make at least two assertions: one, that money is a force to be reckoned with by all people and, second, that God is the supreme force to be followed. God has put money at man's disposal, but the implication is also that man has a responsibility to use money within God's plan. This implies not a hoarding of wealth but rather a view that uses money for the benefit of man.

How Should Christian Ministry Be Funded?

Jesus sent his disciples out, instructing them to "take no gold, nor silver, nor copper in your belts . . . for the laborer deserves his food" (Mt 10:9-10). Christian workers are to expect support from those to whom they minister (Gal 6:6).

Paul reinforces the wisdom behind this in 1 Corinthians 9 where he concludes: "Those who proclaim the gospel should get their living by the gospel" (v. 14). John argues that we should support ministers of the gospel because it makes us "fellow workers in the truth" (3 Jn 8). Through our contributions we stand with them in ministry.

There doesn't appear to be one clear teaching on receiving support from unbelievers. Nehemiah 2 indicates it may be acceptable. King Artaxerxes gave soldiers, supplies and letters of recommendation to Nehemiah. On the other hand, John, though not instructing Gaius to refuse gifts from unbelievers, reports that some workers "have accepted nothing from the heathen" (3 Jn 7).

Christians have argued both sides. One stance is that all money is God's, regardless of who possesses it at the time. To accept a gift from an unbeliever may open the door for us to share more of our ministry, and Jesus Christ, later on. Another view argues that accepting a gift from an unbeliever may leave us open to their influence as to how it is used. In the end, we must decide for ourselves what is appropriate for us and our ministry.

How Did Those in the Bible Raise Support?

God told Aaron (Num 18) that the Levites (the priests of Israel) should be funded by gifts from God's people as they had no other source of revenue. God commanded Moses to take an offering from the people to provide materials for building the tabernacle (Ex 25:1-9). Moses told the people specifically what to bring and how to contribute (Ex 35:5-9). People gave freewill offerings, "from every man whose heart makes him willing" (Ex 25:2).

David contributed generously to the Lord's work, and then asked others, "Who then will offer willingly, consecrating himself today to the LORD?" (1 Chron 29:5). The leaders gave sacrificially first, before the people did.

The church at Antioch took up an offering for famine-struck believers living in Judea (Acts 11:27-30). They sent their gifts to the church elders via Paul and Barnabas. Paul also asked the churches of Galatia and Corinth to contribute to this ministry (1 Cor 16:1-4; Rom 15:25-29).

As a tentmaker, Paul worked to support his ministry (Acts 20:34). At other times he received support from at least one church (Phil 4:14-18). Though it isn't documented that Paul ever asked for support for himself, he frequently taught believers to give to the needs of the saints (2 Cor 8:7). Paul once sent Titus with a well-respected preacher to collect an offering from the church at Corinth. In this way he lent credibility to the offering—uniting it with what the church might label more "spiritual" activities (2 Cor 8—9). Paul also gently persuaded the Corinthian church to give by using the Macedonian church as an example. He compared the two churches hoping that the Corinthians would outdo the Macedonians in the grace of giving.

Do I Have to Have the Gift of Support Raising?

God gives spiritual gifts to individuals. But that does not exempt the rest of us from the responsibility of practicing those gifts. For example, some are blessed with the spiritual gift of helping (1 Cor 12:28). Yet we are all called on to help others. Giving and receiving are likewise practices we are all to follow.

Some will be more gifted in support raising than others. But this does not mean that only fundraisers should go into ministry. Those with special gifts or abilities in this area should perhaps be full-time Christian fundraisers—much like those endowed with the gift of oratory should be preachers. Another approach might be to put those with a special gift in charge of raising support for an entire team. The gift may then be used for the benefit of all.

There are many variables—culture, community, social skills—which help or hinder our ability to raise support. We may also be unable to raise support because we're going about it incorrectly (methods) or because we have a poor attitude. But whether or not we have the gift of fundraising is not the issue. If God has called us to a ministry, then he has also given us the necessary abilities to raise our support.

What Is the Relationship between Praying and Asking for Support?

Jesus instructs us to pray by asking, seeking and knocking (Lk 11:9-10). Such petition keeps our focus on Christ and releases us from anxiety. God cares about us and knows what we need even before we ask (Mt 6:8, 25-33).

Through prayer we seek to discover who we can present our needs to and under what circumstances. Nehemiah prayed for help, and then went out and sought it from the king and the people (Neh 2). We pray for our daily bread, but we don't pray and wait for someone to bring it to us. Paul says working and eating go together (2 Thess 3). Sometimes God answers our prayers through our own actions. The implication is that we have the means to buy food through the earnings from our work. Yet this does not negate the importance of praying for our bread.

God answers prayers through other people. In Exodus 35:4-9 he commands Moses to take an offering from the people. Likewise we should pray for the support we need, ask people to help us in our mission and expect God to answer our prayers through people.

What Is Legitimate Persuasion?

The two extremes of persuasion in support raising are to *not* ask and to manipulate. Can we find a comfortable balance on that continuum?

First, we must realize that asking is a form of persuasion. We have already seen several instances in Scripture where people asked for support. Paul not only asks but applies pressure on Philemon to take care of Onesimus (Philem 8-10). He could only do so because he was a close friend of Philemon. Neither Paul nor we could do the same with strangers.

We are emotional beings. To be truthful about our work and needs we must be emotional and factual. Before the king, Nehemiah shared his sadness and his desire to rebuild Jerusalem (Neh 2). Facts alone don't substantiate our work. After all, to decide to become a Bible translator in Papua New Guinea is an emotional decision; God has touched our heart. The language and feelings we use to describe our mission will play a role in our asking for support. By fully informing and asking others, we're helping them determine where they will support God's work.

What about Giving to the Church and Parachurch Organizations?

Most of the references to giving in the New Testament pertain to giving to the church. It should be the primary receiver of our tithes and offerings. Parachurch work exists only to augment the ministry of the church. Thus, it should only receive support from churches and individuals after the needs of the church have been met. The Bible does give some examples of churches and individuals giving to early parachurch workers, such as Paul, Peter and other itinerant preachers and teachers.

What Makes for Good Relations with Supporters?

Trust. We must consider our supporters as more than a source of gifts to keep our ministry going. When people support our work, they entrust their gifts and prayers to our care. The apostles needed to entrust the waiting on of tables to others (Acts 6:1-4). They didn't have the time or desire to handle every aspect of the ministry. Others were assigned to help.

Accountability. Paul was supported by the church at Philippi and reported back to them what was accomplished through their "partnership." In Philippians 1:1-11 he kept them informed, thanked them and prayed for them. We, too, must remember that our supporters are fellow workers in our ministry.

Sensitivity. In 1 Corinthians 9:1-18 Paul outlines how Christian ministry should be funded—Christian workers have the right to expect support from those they minister to. But in this case he did not ask for it; he saw a possible hindrance to proclaiming the gospel. In another instance (Phil 4:10-19) he accepted a church's gifts. Why? Paul was sensitive to his audience. He saw the Corinthians were too weak in their handling of money and ministry for him to accept support. Their wrong attitudes regarding what they should receive if they paid for Paul's support would prevent them from clearly seeing the gospel. On the other hand, Paul accepted a gift from the Philippian church since it furthered their growth (Phil 4:17). So too we must be sensitive when placing expectations for giving on potential supporters. Sensitivity and concern work both ways in our support relationships.

3

A Brief History of Missionary Funding

Support raising is not a new idea. Hundreds of thousands of missionaries have gone before us using a variety of methods to obtain funds for ministry.

The Early Church to the Reformation
True missionary support began with Jesus. He was given food and shelter by followers as early beneficiaries of his teaching. They contributed out of their own means (Lk 8:1-3).

Paul was one of the first to openly encourage church and individual giving. During part of his ministry, he decided to labor with his own hands for his support. But he noted that other apostles, including Peter and the brothers of Jesus, were maintained by the churches (1 Cor 9:3-7). Paul began one of the first relief efforts when he raised money from the gentile churches to help the poorer Judean Christians. He encouraged giving by recommending they set aside something on the first day of each week (1 Cor 16:2). This form of systematic giving is similar to the requests for monthly support that we often see.

Priests in fourth-century Europe gained their support by combining an Old Testament and an early Christian teaching and turning them into a command for the people to bring firstfruits (wine, grain and animals) and one-tenth of all income to the church.

Every true prophet or teacher who came to a Christian community was also supported.

Prior to Constantine, the first Christian Roman emperor, priests were expected to perform certain public duties to help cover the cost of their ministry. But they found the double duty of ministry and work burdensome. Early in the fourth century, Constantine exempted clergy from these public obligations. Instead, a form of inheritance (legacies) to the church was instituted. This was perhaps the earliest form of a tax-exempt gift permitted by a government. But by the close of the fifth century the practice had gone sour. Some of the clergy were accused of using illegal means to obtain legacies from the wealthy.

Some cite Constantine's formation of a state church as the beginning of problems with voluntary giving. As the Roman Catholic Church grew, it needed more money. Well-meaning methods were introduced to encourage people to give. The Church, with its teaching of merit by works, prepared the way for the actual sale of spiritual worth, the sale of escape from punishment for sin (indulgences), and even the sale of church offices (simony). Then, as now, some thought they could buy spiritual rewards or favor from God. But as methods of funding grew shrewder, the laity became less willing to support the church financially.

The Reformation did not change the laity's attitudes. Reformers felt the people were still unwilling to voluntarily give to the church. All over post-Reformation Europe, church and state combined powers to raise church funds through tithing laws and state support. Quaker, Separatist and Anabaptist advocates of voluntaryism were actually persecuted for resisting such laws in the sixteenth and seventeenth centuries.

Giving and the New World
Advocates of voluntary mission support were in the minority when they arrived in the New World. In fact, involuntary church support was one of the first laws adopted by the new Commonwealth of Massachusetts. The Plymouth Colony Founders (the Pilgrims) and

the Massachusetts Bay Founders (the Puritans) dissented. Thus the cycle of legislation leading to poor giving and more legislation continued. As a result, people became even more alienated from the organized church.

States were forced to abandon compulsory support laws by the end of the eighteenth century, largely because of successful fundraising by new voluntary Christian efforts. But the procedures that took their place were nothing new. These included the sale or rental of pew space to families, lotteries, subscription (pledge) lists, church-farm ownership, and buying and selling of goods in the church.

During the last half of the eighteenth century and the first half of the nineteenth century, a great spiritual awakening took place in Europe and America which led to the formation of the first modern mission organizations. Leaders in this movement emphasized organizing *around* God's work. John Wesley was one such innovator. He divided his followers into cell groups, or classes, and collected voluntary funds from them to aid social concerns.

Other such volunteer groups were the missionary societies. One of the first formed in the London suburb of Clapham, where several wealthy Anglican businessmen made their home. The Clapham Sect (as they became known) worked individually and together in support of religious and philanthropic projects.

Groups such as the Society for the Propagation of the Gospel in New England, the Society for Promoting Christian Knowledge, Moravian societies, and the British and Foreign Bible Society also sprang up during this time. This marked the beginning of the Protestant foreign missionary enterprise. Most societies were supported by individuals; some were actual extensions of Protestant denominations. The London Missionary Society (formerly the Missionary Society) drew its funds and personnel chiefly from Congregationalists, the strongest of the early American denominations. The Methodists and Baptists organized their own societies shortly thereafter.

William Carey's mission to India was one of the forerunners of modern missions. His funding policies had their roots in faith mission work. He favored voluntary, rather than church or state-garnered, support. One of the earliest faith mission agencies was the China Inland Mission (CIM), founded by Hudson Taylor in 1886. Their principles—never ask for money, never tell anyone except God of your needs and look to God through prayer to support your needs—probably stemmed from disdain for church fundraising policies. While CIM (now Overseas Missionary Fellowship) still adheres to these principles, most faith agencies today ask for funds or make their needs openly known.

Students were among the first to encourage American Protestant missions to go into the world by forming the American Board of Commissioners for Foreign Missions. They were funded by a variety of church denominations, particularly the Congregationalists and Presbyterians. By the late nineteenth and early twentieth centuries, American Protestantism had begun supplying the majority of funds and personnel for foreign missions. European church support for missions continued. Churches in England and like-minded circles in Germany began funding such projects as a school to train youth for missionary service.

As America expanded, clergy moved west without support from eastern churches. They took up farming, working six days a week for family support, and then preached on Sundays. Voluntary gifts from those they ministered to soon enabled them to devote more time to pastoring. Early Methodist pastors in Europe and the United States adapted to the situation by becoming circuit riders. Most lived in poverty, traveling from church to church to preach the gospel.

Some foreign missions were able to attract personnel and funds with the help of an inspirational—even heroic—leader. Such was the case with Hudson Taylor, George Müller and Dwight L. Moody. Their zeal and openness in ministry attracted funds and volunteers for pioneering missions.

Taylor and Müller are well known for extreme humility regarding contributions to their work. Taylor vowed never to go into debt.

As a result, he guaranteed no salaries for his coworkers:

> We might, indeed, have had a guarantee fund if we had wished it; but we felt it to be unnecessary, and likely to do harm. Not only is money given from mixed motives to be dreaded; money wrongly placed may also prove a serious hindrance to spiritual work, especially should it lead to confidence of any to rest in the material rather than the spiritual, the finite rather than the infinite supply. We can afford to have as little as the Lord may see fit to give, but we cannot afford to have unconsecrated money or money in wrong positions. (*The Story of the China Inland Mission,* vol. 1, p. 236)

Contrary to Taylor's rejection of unconsecrated money, General William Booth, founder of the Salvation Army, once said, "I will accept any kind of money—even the Devil's. I'll wash it in the blood of Christ and use it for the glory of God!"

George Müller's radical belief that only God should be asked to supply funds for his orphanage was compromised only once. That was in early September 1938 when his funds were depleted. Describing the situation as a "solemn crisis," Müller gathered his staff to explain their need in detail—his first and only time. Together they prayed and miraculously received the money.

Asking and giving have played a dual role in the history of missions. Some of the best-known missions pioneers were also among the greatest givers. Before leaving England for China at age twenty-three, C. T. Studd learned he was to inherit a large sum of money in two years from his father's will. At that moment he decided he would give it all to missions. Two years later, on January 13, 1887, Studd wrote checks to D. L. Moody, Hudson Taylor, George Müller, William Booth and others, totaling what he estimated to be a twenty-nine thousand pound inheritance. He later found his estimate to be short by several thousand pounds, and gave that away as well.

William Borden, a young man deeply touched by the volunteer movement, freely gave of his family's wealth. In his three years at Princeton Seminary he contributed $70,000 to Christian work. By the time of his death in 1913, the twenty-five-year-old Borden had supplied his church and various missions with over one and a half million dollars—his entire inheritance.

John Wesley's philosophy about giving was, "Make all you can. Save all you can. Give away all you can." And he did. In the first year of his ministry Wesley's income was thirty pounds. He kept twenty-eight and gave away two. The next year it increased to sixty pounds. He kept twenty-eight and gave away thirty-two. The third year he made one hundred twenty pounds—keeping twenty-eight and giving the rest away.

Support Raising in the Twentieth Century

At the beginning of the twentieth century, state support of the Roman Catholic Church in Europe began to wane. Substantial gifts from the wealthy gave way to comparatively small donations from thousands of lay people. Never had the Church had so many professional missionaries supported by so many devoted Church members. By 1914 additional aid was coming from the Roman Catholic Churches in the United States and other countries outside of Europe.

The proliferation of parachurch groups beginning in the early 1900s had also forced a change in Protestant church funding. Parachurch groups, because of their reliance on communicating needs, became well versed in raising funds. They raised their funds personally, regularly cycling their missionaries through the supporting churches.

Mainline denominations tried to become better organized and established central missions funds to which satellite churches were required to contribute. Missionaries in these denominations were supported by the central fund, freeing them from personal support raising. But this centralization had its problems. Since denominational missionaries didn't have to raise personal support, member churches rarely saw the people they were funding, and interest declined. Based on how they raise support, Protestant missionaries today tend to fall into one of three categories. Those affiliated with faith missions belong to the Interdenominational Foreign Missions Association (IFMA). Many of the smaller, more conservative denominational missions belong to the Evangelical Foreign Missions Association (EFMA). Some members of the EFMA expect their people to raise their support before leaving on their mission. A third category is churches or denominations that completely underwrite the cost of their missionaries.

Churches and parachurch groups have grown more interdependent in the past several decades. Churches have often found themselves competing with other groups for funds and personnel. Opportunities and resources from both sides must be pooled if there is to be an adequate missions outreach. Though the growth of parachurch groups is subsiding, their increasing need for funds places more and more requests before the evangelical community.

The missions enterprise has come a long way since the early church, though there has been little "new under the sun" when it comes to missionary funding. Voluntary and forced giving have both taken turns in popularity. Voluntaryism in the early church gave way to the impersonal giving laws of the state church. Today, even with voluntary giving, things are considerably more complex. Depending on where they are on the mission field, between $25,000 and $35,000 is needed to support a family of four. And this figure continues to rise. Funding methods vary from state-supplemented work in some parts of Africa to full-time "tentmaking" missions in the Middle East and China. Throughout history, missionaries have adapted regardless of the situation—ensuring the support needed to carry the gospel forward.

4

Your Agency, Job Description and Budget

When Jim accepted his position, he was greeted by a downpour of papers and instructions. The deluge began with a job description. Then came more papers about the agency—history, procedures and so forth. He knew they must be important but wondered how he was to sort them all out.

Jim felt relieved when he was told that the main thing for preparing for support raising was to know and accept his organization's purposes and goals. That sounded simple. He knew his agency was sending him to Alaska to do programming for a gospel radio station. "What more do I need to know?" he wondered. "I've been running a station here for the past five years—I know what this job is about."

So Jim proceeded to contact people to raise his $18,000 support goal. But he never realized he'd get so many questions about the agency he had joined.

"People asked me about things I'd never heard of," he said. "Ministry teams in Latin America, gospel tracts used in local churches—I never realized I was joining such a diverse ministry."

Knowing Your Agency

Knowing our agency's broad goals and specific ministries will help us effectively present our work to the public. The Boy Scouts are right—we need to be prepared.

If we are required to raise one hundred per cent of our support, we need to know how that follows from our organization's purposes. We need to know the connection between our agency's philosophy of support raising and how that is translated into staff procedures. In most organizations support requirements exist so that employees can single-mindedly devote themselves to ministry. The requirement is usually borne out of an understanding of scriptural guidelines, our culture and the mission's task. To split our attention between ministry and an outside job is to possibly decrease the effectiveness of our ministry. For example, Ellen, a missionary to high-school students, finds she is able to devote more time to students when she has raised her financial support than when she holds a job to cover expenses. If she had a job, it would have to be part time. And part-time jobs don't usually pay enough to cover costs. So chances are she would probably have to raise support anyway just to supplement her other income.

There are exceptions to this practice. Some inner-city pastors and missionaries find it necessary to have an outside job—either for survival or to identify with the people they minister to or both. For them, raising support is not an option.

Whatever our situation, we need to know our agency's philosophy behind raising support.

Likewise, we must know what portion of our support is used for administration and how these funds are used. And more importantly, we need to honestly ask ourselves, Do I agree with this practice and how the funds are divided? Attitudes vary widely on this topic. Many are turned off by the thought of raising administrative or overhead costs, and yet they aren't sure why. Different organizations have different philosophies. More will be said later in this chapter on the topic. For now, if you have questions, speak with your supervisor or someone in your organization who can explain its policies and practices. Get the whole story before a negative attitude clouds your support ministry.

These points about attitude and purpose may seem elementary.

But we've witnessed again and again that without stated and agreed-to purposes etched in their minds, new Christian workers flounder in support raising, eventually becoming emotionally drained and burned-out. Appointees released in this state are poor advertisements for the joyful calling to God's ministry. Good training, close supervision and clearly delineated roles and purposes are essential to keep this from happening.

The Job Description and Budget

Having a call to minister is a beginning. Several other elements come into play in moving us from our call to our work. One of these elements is finding partners to support us. We must be able to translate our desire into terms understood by those we seek as supporters. Having a clear job description and budget will help.

Job descriptions, by nature, constantly grow and change. Yet they remain tangible reminders of the tasks that lie before us. Our job description needs to outline more than a geographic region but less than a schedule for each day's activities. This gives us a sense of direction, and comforts us about the mission ahead. We also need an understandable version for our supporters so they will know what we will be doing. We mention "understandable" because frequently we get caught up in the language of our organization and pay little attention to how outsiders view us. We must help our supporters by translating our job description into terms they can understand.

Many overseas assignments aren't easily put into a job description. Erin was headed to Italy to work with youth but had no idea what she would specifically be doing until she actually started. All she could tell her supporters was that she would be sharing the gospel with Italian students. We can work with our supervisors to get at least a simple paragraph or two that describes what we will do. It should mention our attainable goals and how we will be held accountable.

We also need a complete budget. People want to know what we'll be doing and what it will cost. Individuals and churches usually request a few basic figures from Christian workers.

First is salary. How much will you receive each month to cover living expenses for you and your family?

Next are benefits. How much medical insurance does your supporting agency provide? Do they offer a retirement or pension plan? Any life or other emergency insurance? Itemize, then state the combined amount for all benefits.

Then comes travel and expenses. How much can you spend for furloughs, conferences or visits to various work locations? If you serve overseas, tell how often you return on furlough and what portion of your yearly budget covers it.

Then there is *overhead,* the term we often use when referring to office, accounting, supervisory and gift-receipting expenses. Is there a percentage or flat amount of your budget used to cover such administrative expenses? All Christian service agencies have overhead. In some there are as many as three geographic levels of overhead expense. Area, regional and national services are provided to increase the effectiveness and efficiency of the Christian worker.

A few organizations don't charge administrative costs to their workers. These costs are instead covered by other income sources. Still other agencies take a percentage of each worker's budget for national or local office expenses.

Inter-Varsity Christian Fellowship staff are charged a set figure for services which they and their supporters receive. Several times a year we receive calls from Inter-Varsity staff or their supporters who are disappointed in our overhead system. Most of the time their frustrations stem from a misunderstanding which we can easily clear up.

We must know, endorse and be able to explain our organization's administrative charges. Supporters need to understand that overhead is not merely money sent off to some faraway office. Rather, it is an expense which frees us from hours of work: keeping careful records for the IRS, issuing receipts for supporters and so forth. When others are hired to handle these tasks we are able to devote more time to our ministry.

The most essential part of administrative costs belongs to supervision. Where would we be without time spent learning about cross-cultural work, basic ministry skills and problem solving from an experienced supervisor in our agency? We would have to fend for ourselves. Few pastors or businesspeople could last long without the supportive help of secretaries and accountants. Neither could we. We should write an explanation of the costs of administration as part of our budget. Supervisors can answer questions about the overhead items built into the budget. We won't be effective advocates or support-raisers if we can't agree with the allocations. (See the sample budget in figure 4.1.)

We can also include special expenses we will incur. Some workers have a special travel allotment as part of their total budget. This also needs to be written into the budget.

The budget categories should be added into one figure—the bottom line. We like to state ours as a monthly amount as well.

Sample Budget

Salary	$11,700	This is my first-year salary, paid on a monthly basis.
FICA, Workman's Comp. Insurance	$940	Required government insurance programs and $50 for national emergency fund for staff.
Medical Insurance	$2,150	Coverage for my entire family.
Travel & Training	$3,000	Travel reimbursed at 20¢ per mile; training includes summer orientation and special regional events.
Telephone & Supplies	$350	Business calls and expenses for writing you and other supporters.
National Administration	$3,000	For supervision, accounting, gift receipting, payroll, insurance claims and government financial reports.
Area Administration	$1,000	For supervision, training and services from the area office (varies by area).
TOTAL BUDGET	$22,140	Includes all my expenses for one year ($1,845 per month).

Figure 4.1   This sample budget helps a potential supporter understand how his or her gift will be used.

Needs stated in monthly terms help when seeking monthly contributions. Quoting a monthly figure also lessens the impact of a large budget.

Beneath the total figure write any support received so far. Sometimes the newly appointed missionary knows in advance that his or her parents have pledged one hundred dollars a month. By subtracting the amount raised thus far we let our potential supporter know we're on our way. What's left is what we are seeking to raise.

Finally, some supporters will ask how their gift will be used—"What assurance do I have that all $15 will go to Rick's support?" This is an important question to answer because it raises issues of integrity and trust in an organization. But it's also tricky, especially if we try to answer it by presenting our budget. We should explain that our agency, like all nonprofit organizations, is required by law to spend each gift on the specific person or project for which it was intended. The confusion comes when a donor's gift arrives with no specific or an unclear designation. By right, that gift can be spent anywhere it is needed within the organization. Most Christian organizations even raise funds for the category "where most needed" on a local or national level. This gives them the freedom to allocate funds for emergencies, new projects, administration and even deficits.

So if one supporter gives a gift earmarked for you, he or she can be assured it will be used for your mission. But if the gift designation is not clearly noted, it will be used where the ministry needs it most.

Before we launch into planning and raising our support, we should ask our supervisor about questions and concerns that have come up in the past. Learning from those who went before us can be the best way to prevent problems and confusion.

Attitude and purposes, job description and budget must all be clear. We must be prepared to explain them to the skeptical businessman, our grandmother, an inquiring missions committee and most importantly to ourselves.

Next Steps

1. Obtain a job description which outlines the responsibilities, goals, authority and supervision you will have in your position.

2. Talk to your predecessor or a coworker regarding the "finer points" they feel you might need to know about your ministry.

3. Ask your supervisor for a detailed budget, including a list and description of categories included, as well as specific costs of each. Find out what contingencies exist when your budget is in deficit or surplus.

5

Defining Your Audiences

Earlier we touched on a point we now need to embrace. People are the heart of our support-raising mission. They are the ones who encourage us with their support. They are the ones we can confide in, the people who believe in what we're doing. For these reasons and more, we need to know our audiences—their likes and dislikes—and handle them with respect. We are seeking partners in our ministry.

We need to identify who we know, who might support our work and what personal characteristics they have. Right now, this group is probably only a few names and faces in your mind. There's Mom and Dad, two former roommates and a classmate in Bible college. This chapter will help you expand the list.

We've divided this task into three parts: listing potential supporters, segmenting the list and record keeping. There are exercises and forms included to assist you in the process. The task seems awesome, but taking the time to follow this procedure now will point you in the right direction and save you headaches later.

Listing Potential Supporters
If we're serious about the call and scope of our ministry, we'll want

to include as many people on our list as possible. At this stage, we can't assume whether or not someone will support the work. We must remember to list all those who can support us financially and prayerfully.

On a separate sheet of paper begin listing everyone you know by the following categories (there is no need to duplicate names over several categories):

family members (immediate and distant)
in-laws
personal friends
church friends
past school friends
your pastor(s) (your current, former and parents')
teachers
college fellowship alums
neighbors
parents' friends
parents' business associates
work associates
service organizations, such as:
    Christian Businessmen's Club
    Christian Women's Missionary Society
    Christian Women's Club
    Women Aglow
    Pastor's circle
    Community prayer breakfast
    Four Square Gospelmen's Association
    Full Gospel Businessmen's Association
    Kiwanis
    Rotary
 other staff and their supporters (your predecessor's mailing list)
 your Christmas card list

At some point have your spouse or a friend look at the list and suggest additions. Obtain permission from family members before adding any of their friends or acquaintances to the list.

Segmenting the List

The goal in segmenting the list is to isolate groups of people according to their relationship to you or their motivation to support you. For example, family members support you because they care about *you*. Beneficiaries of your organization might support you because you represent the group that led them to Christ. Members of your church might give and pray because they consider you their missionary.

There are a variety of methods to divide the list. Find the largest groupings and try to efficiently organize them according to the amount and type of your contact with them. One way to do this is by dividing the list by the people's relationship to you. Your friends have a different orientation to you as a missionary than your family does. Having three to four homogeneous groups will facilitate more personal communication. Most find the clearest divisions among friends, family, pastors and churches, and all others.

Thomas is a pilot who, when raising his support, realized he had a peculiar problem. Most of his friends and family were not believers. He decided that if he was ever to make it into his mission he would need the support of his unbelieving friends. So that's how he divided his list—between Christians and non-Christians.

So far we've mentioned segmentation which will involve sending different messages. One other way to subdivide the list of contacts is geographically. Dividing the list between people living close by and far away will require different forms of contact—visits versus letters. (This will be covered more specifically in chapter nine.)

Some will also have a better understanding of your mission and agency than others. You might divide your initial contact between those two groups. For one group, a lengthy description of the purpose of your organization would sound odd ("I already know this"). Write or speak to each group at their own level of understanding. Don't assume everyone has heard of the agency. Some may think they know the organization and disagree with its methods or purposes. You may not overcome their objections, but you'll do your organization a major service by answering their complaints. Keep in touch with complainers—over time your good performance may change their opinion.

In general we want to divide our contacts into groups which facilitate more personal communication. But it can be overdone. We should try to strike a balance between personableness and expediency.

Keeping Records

Now we need to decide how to file and keep track of the names. We should adopt and use a comfortable record-keeping system before we begin asking for support. If we're fortunate enough to have access to a personal computer, we can use its word-processing capability to list and organize names.

For those without computer access, we recommend using the Support Record format (see figure 5.1). All pertinent information is on a single page for each supporter. The entire support list can then be kept in a three-ring binder, with other support materials and gift print-outs. Transfer each name from the general list to a Record sheet. Include their current address, home and work phone numbers, name of spouse, occupation and how the person was referred to you (for example, Dad's coworker). With a large list, keeping accurate and correctly spelled information is especially important. We can easily remember details on friends and family, but when we add friends of friends, or church members, we need written reminders.

Two other bits of information we should keep on these sheets are finances (Have they pledged support? How much? How often?) and communication (When was the last contact? What type was it? What was communicated?). Some workers keep track of supporters' birthdays, children (and ages), church and church responsibilities (for instance, missions committee), pastor or other interests. Anything we might refer to in later correspondence, we should begin collecting now.

Once the sheets are completed, place them in alphabetical

SUPPORT RECORD

Date support started: _____

Name_____ Spouse _____

Home address: _____ Office address: _____

_____

_____

Phone: _____ Phone: _____

Church: _____ Pastor: _____

Personal notes (family, interests, etc.) _____

_____

_____

_____

_____

GIVING RECORD

	Pledge Amt.	Jan.	Feb.	Mar.	Apr.	May	Jun.	Jul.	Aug.	Sep.	Oct.	Nov.	Dec.	Total
1985														
1986														
1987														
1988														
1989														

COMMUNICATION RECORD

Notes, Letters to and from, Gifts, etc.: _____

_____

_____

_____

_____

_____

_____

PRAYER RECORD

Date	Prayer Request	Answer

Paste
Photo
Here

Figure 5.1   The Support Record is one way you can keep pertinent information on each of your supporters. Keep each sheet updated and store them in a three-ring binder with the rest of your support-raising information.

order in a three-ring binder with the rest of the support-training materials and gift print-outs. Keep extra sheets on hand for adding names referred to you by other supporters.

The Support Records help us keep basic information on each of our supporters. Another tool we recommend is the Support Team Chart. This summarizes the information on the Support Records onto one page. It lets us know where we stand financially compared to our monthly goal. It serves as a reminder to thank supporters for their gifts—ideally, that should occur as often as each person sends in a gift. From the Chart we'll be able to see at a glance who has forgotten to send in their regular gift. (One missed gift is understandable. If they've missed two, call or send a note of reminder.) And finally, we can mark new pledges and increased gifts—both call for a personal thank you.

The Team Chart is very simple to fill out and interpret (see figure 5.2). Most agencies provide their staff with a monthly computer print-out of supporters, their gifts and the dates of the gifts. Transfer the gift amounts onto both charts as soon as the print-outs are received. Write the names of the supporters in alphabetical order, skipping lines so that new names can be added later. Write your annual and monthly financial goals in the upper left-hand blanks. Be sure to know what each person's monthly pledge is before writing an assumed amount in the left-hand column. If a person has chosen to pledge $30 bimonthly, write in $30/6. Or if the gift is quarterly, $30/4. This way blank spaces for certain months will be expected.

Each time we send a letter to our supporters, we should record the date sent in the row marked *Letter*. This will show how regular we are in keeping in contact with supporters. At the bottom of the page there are two codes. A dot (.) should be put in the month each person has either started or increased their pledge. Each pledging supporter should be asked to increase his or her pledge on an annual basis. Why? For one, our budget will undoubtedly increase on an annual basis. And rather than constantly seek new supporters to fill the gap, we should first go to those who already

SUPPORT TEAM CHART

Year

monthly goal $ _____
annual goal $ _____

		Jul	Aug	Sep	Oct	Nov	Dec	6 mo. avg.	Jan	Feb	Mar	Apr	May	Jun	12 mo. avg.
(date)	Letter														
($)	Monthly Total														

Pledge	Name														

• pledge anniversary   *special contact (personal thank you, visit, etc.)

Figure 5.2   *The Support Team Chart portrays both monthly and year-to-date totals for your supporters' giving. It shows you at a glance not only how your income is meeting expenses, but also how frequently you are making contact with people.*

support us. Chances are, the people supporting us will either get a raise or change their giving patterns or both on a yearly basis. By asking, we're helping them make their decision.

The other mark is an asterisk (*) used to denote any special contact we've had with a supporter. Visits, phone calls, personal cards and special gifts come under this category. Both of us have been embarrassed by our poor memories when a supporter thanked us for a gift. "What gift?" we thought. "The book you sent me earlier last month—remember?" Oops.

Keep all print-outs, record sheets and copies of correspondence with the other support-raising materials in a three-ring binder. In this way you'll know where everything is for your support ministry. The forms can be revised and combined to meet particular styles and situations. We don't mean to make record keeping complex or tedious. The point is to keep helpful records from the outset. Though they will never see our forms, supporters will know we care about them if we keep and make use of accurate records.

Next Steps

1. Make enough copies of Support Records and Support Team Charts to handle everyone on your list (and more). Buy a three-ring binder with pockets to keep all support records in one place.

2. Each time you receive a print-out of gifts, take time to record the gifts and any changes (addresses, phone numbers, etc.) onto your forms.

6

Communication— Your Messages

In the last two chapters we discussed support from your point of view—describing your calling, position and requirements. Here we will show how to outline and present your mission and need in a context your audience will understand. We'll look at people—their interests and concerns, their likes and dislikes— and why some might support us. Also, we'll see how to translate our ministry and needs into a *case statement* for support.

Many people think their powers of communication are too feeble to rally support. That's not true. We don't need to be charismatic leaders or have an out-of-the-ordinary ministry to raise support. What we do need is to pray for guidance and work to contact people. God will enable us to fulfill the mission for which he has chosen us.

Knowing Your Audience

You have segmented your support list into three or four homogeneous groups, recognizing that each group—family, friends, churches, organizations and so on—has its own way of relating to you and your agency. Now you must identify what is unique to each group and gear your presentation to those characteristics.

Take your closest friends, for example. Chances are, they're already sold on you—who you are and what you plan to do with your life. Friends trust us—they know us and have confidence in us. Now you must try to figure out what it is about you that would prompt your friends to support you in ministry. Reversing roles might help—why would you support one of them? Friends support friends because they care about them. Whatever greater purpose or value the mission agency extols is really second in importance to them. Usually, a friend already trusts your judgment in choosing, or being chosen by, a ministry. The point is you can dispense with lengthy generalizations and formal language. *You* are the credible endorsement for the mission. You should emphasize the reasons why they might support you in the presentation.

Other segments of your audience have different concerns. Some may be concerned about the direction of today's youth. As a Youth for Christ staff person you would want to highlight the positive effect you hope to have with high-school students. Family may be more concerned with your specific calling. Pastors may care more about how your ministry complements theirs.

Packaging Your Message

People not only pay attention to certain content, they also get their messages through particular channels. We should be aware of people's likes and dislikes regarding means of communication. For all the criticism leveled at television as a medium, one can't ignore the fact that almost everyone watches it. What does this mean for us? Most people digest shorter, more visual messages. This becomes more apparent when we look at the newspaper and magazine formats people buy most. Correspondingly, our letters and literature should be short, personal and visually interesting. We should look at the styles most often used, and then ask ourselves how we can put our mission and support messages into a format that will be noticed and effective.

We must also consider the language we use with our audiences. Words carry powerful stereotypes. For example, to many the word *missionary* conjures thoughts of a sweaty white man with pith helmet and dog-eared Bible in hand. To a pastor the word may mean "overseas." To a parent, "low pay." The point is, we cannot assume people will understand who we are or what we plan to do. We must choose our words and analogies carefully.

People tend to show their professionalism by the jargon of their work. Christian workers are no different. The result can alienate our audiences. We can never successfully use acronyms or abbreviations with our audiences. It defeats the purpose of communication. We must also be sensitive to the language of *evangelicalism*. That word alone can mean ten things to ten different people. We must consider our audience before we write or speak. Using the definition of a word or a title rather than the word itself reverses this trend of exclusive language and makes us better understood and appreciated.

Four simple points will help us remember to keep our messages appropriate to our audience. First, we should *listen* to our (potential) supporters, being sensitive to their likes, dislikes, language and so on. Second, we should *consider* what factors make various means of communication effective, especially noticing what we appreciate in the correspondence we receive from missionaries we support. Third, we should *speak* directly and personally to our audience in a language they can understand (let a friend critique the support presentation or letter). Finally, we should *record* the interests and concerns of those who support us so we can address these areas in our correspondence.

Giving, Asking and Thanking

There is an inherent human need to *give*. God created us in his image—to love, to share, to be gracious toward one another. Also, we need to be needed by others. There's a bond formed or strengthened by giving that makes us feel accepted.

It is also important to know the reasons why people need to give. Like it or not, people will support us for different reasons.

In 2 Corinthians 8 and 9 Paul teaches that people should give because they love Christ. We want to be obedient to him, so we give. Others realize they can't do what we've been called to do, so they give vicariously. Some people just want to be partners in something worthwhile—like sharing Jesus the Messiah with Jewish people. Related to this, some supporters give because they see a need. Paul also mentions giving as an example to others.

There are other, more psychological reasons we should be aware of. People often give to boost their own feelings of self-worth. We feel capable, willing and generous about what we're doing. Others give to perpetuate their interests. We know of one person who will give to almost anything that aids the people of India. The Lord has given him a consuming passion that is satisfied when he helps.

As long as we're talking about needs, we should mention asking for support. Asking is the link between our need and the supporters' need to give. We can learn the how-to's, we can plan and we can pray, but the one thing we must do is ask people to help us. As mentioned in chapter two, we often forget that God answers prayer *through* people. God has called you to serve at Oregon State, and you need to raise $24,000 a year to do it; wouldn't he also designate people with the resources you need? We must overcome our own passivity in this area and learn how to become grateful receivers.

We live in a busy, complex, need-cluttered world. Our potential supporters must hear our specific request above the din.

As Christian workers, we need to show appreciation to those who support us. People should be thanked out of gratitude—without their help we wouldn't be able to do the Lord's work. Thankfulness is a command given in several places in Scripture (Phil 4:6; Col 4:2; 1 Thess 5:18). People need encouragement to know that they are doing the right thing. Few things are more bothersome than to hear a person say he or she doesn't have time to thank supporters. That's an excuse, not a reason. God wants us to nurture relationships with our supporters. We strengthen our bonds with them by offering and receiving thanks.

Preparing Your Personal Case Statement
Many names have been given to what we call the case statement.

Preparing the case statement is simply bringing together all the elements we've discussed so far—job description, budget, segmented support list, principles of communication—into a concise audience-centered presentation. It is a description of your ministry, your need and your specific request put into the potential supporter's language.

The case statement may be applied to many situations. It can be developed for an individual, a ministry team, a conference or an entire organization. We will cover two types—the personal and team case statement.

We have been called into ministry, and we seek support from people referred to as our supporters. But this poses a dilemma. Should *we* really be the object of people's support? Rarely. Looking again at Paul and the other apostles, we see that they saw themselves as ministers in need, not emphasizing glory for themselves but seeking to glorify Jesus Christ. Without being too self-depreciating, we should carry a similar torch. Before developing our case statement, we need to check to see that we emphasize our role *in light of our agency or team effort.* The distinction is subtle but real. We need to remember in all aspects of ministry: "more of Christ, less of me." This attitude will also keep us from feeling rejected should some choose not to give.

Before we begin writing the personal case statement, we should think about our particular situation and background. We must consider the level of familiarity our audiences have with us, our ministry, mission field and agency. Sometimes we in Inter-Varsity become so involved in our work that we assume everyone is concerned about the faith of college students. *Don't assume anything!* Few people will understand the totality of our ministry without an explanation. A case statement is always presented in the language of the person or group to whom it is being given. People empathize best when they hear a message they don't have to translate.

Seven basic questions are answered in the personal case statement. Adapt them to your situation.

1. What need exists for your ministry? Whether you'll be working with college students or expatriate Bengali workers in London, describe your mission field. Explain briefly who and where they are.

2. Why should I support you or your organization? Are you the only person or agency reaching these people? Do you have particular abilities or experience that will better equip you to serve? There is a danger here of comparing groups and being brash. The point is that you chose your agency for important reasons. Mention those reasons.

3. What do you hope to achieve in your mission? Don't be shy in answering this. State your greatest ambitions with all the enthusiasm that carries you into the field. Stay away from dryly stated goals. People want to know what a typical end product of your work will be. For example, how do you hope your students will glorify God after graduation?

4. What is your (total) ministry cost? Money isn't the only factor here. Perhaps you're passing up graduate school, seminary (for now), or some other opportunity. Lend importance to your decision by stating what the cost will be. Your mission endeavor will also need a blanket of prayer from faithful partners. Perhaps you can let others know specifically how you want to be upheld in prayer. (For an example of how you might present your budget, see page 30.)

5. How soon do you need to raise all of your support? This is a financial question your supervisor can answer. If you expect to be on the field by a certain time, even if it's as soon as possible, give your audience a target date.

6. What are you asking of me? When presenting your case in a letter, this is as far as you should go. We encourage people to rarely ask for money in a letter. Perhaps instead you could tell the reader you plan to call to get together and discuss how he or she can help (see chapter seven). Be specific at this point in your presentation. Perhaps you need $20,000 to go overseas. How might that be broken down for others' involvement? A first step is to put the total into a monthly amount—$1,800. Then you can say you are looking for sixty people to give thirty dollars a month.

7. *What will (or will not) happen if you aren't able to go?* This is just the converse of question three and may or may not be needed. Usually put in a closing statement; this may lend greater urgency to your mission. For example, Christian student leaders will be without the encouragement they need, or, plans for church planting in Mexico will be postponed. The point is that *something* will be held up, changed or lessened when you can't be on the mission field.

Analogies are often helpful in describing a mission or agency to an unfamiliar public. For example, few know what an Inter-Varsity staff member does on campus. But almost everyone knows what a church youth pastor does. The two are similar and can be described as such. We can adapt our case presentation for parents, a pastor, close friends and so on. Each case statement should take into account their perceptions. We can't begin talking to people about support until our thoughts are gathered and these questions answered.

The Team Case Statement
The major difference between personal and team statements lies in their scope. The personal case is largely for the benefit of the Christian worker whom it describes and can be used in a variety of contexts. The team case is a multipage document used in face-to-face presentations. It is a detailed plan, complete with goals, staff, costs and timetables.

Ideally, agencies will put together an organizational purpose and case statement, and have members or teams in the organization produce a personal case which stems from it. This method of combining personal and team case statements allows you the freedom to selectively highlight the information most relevant to the particular audience you're addressing.

For example, World Vision's international purpose is met through the work of people involved in one of several diverse ministries. Ted, a cameraman for a film crew working on a television special on hunger relief in Kenya, is able to explain his role to supporters in two ways. To his family and friends, Ted can emphasize himself and his work—a cameraman gifted and chosen by God to portray world needs to those who can help meet them— and relate this to the broad goals of World Vision. To unfamiliar church committees, he can emphasize the wide-ranging work of World Vision, its effectiveness and integrity, and then relate how supporting him would further the work of the organization. With both groups he can use the same case statement highlighting different pages.

We've found that the most effective team case moves from the general to the specific. It starts with the broad purposes of the mission, moving to specific goals, then past accomplishments, particular programs, future projects and finally, finances and support needs. In the section on programs you can insert a description of your particular ministry. Also, in the section on support needs you can either add or substitute your individual financial requirements and possible ways to give. Obviously, this is a flexible document which can be adjusted to fit the type of presentation you're giving.

The team or agency case statement should be a group venture. If it is not already written, then as many people as will use the case should be involved in putting it together. People can describe their agency's case more easily if they have been involved in its concept and writing.

We mentioned that the team case is also printed and presented to individual supporters. This need not be fancy, but it should be neat and well copied. We suggest that at least the cover (with the theme statement) should be professionally designed and printed. Each topic listed below should be on a separate, single page. The writing should be brief and the information easily accessible. The following is a suggested outline for producing an agency or team case:

1. *The Theme.* A brief three- to five-word summary statement

that captures the mission idea of the organization. This will be the title page with your name and/or the name of the organization.

2. *The Mission.* What is the general purpose of the organization?

3. *The Goals.* Stated in personal terms, what does the organization want to see happen? Generally, how is the mission going to be accomplished?

4. *The Program.* State the quantifiable objectives for a specific period of time—both for the organization (nationally or internationally) and for localized areas or divisions. What are the chief programs?

5. *The Impact or Accomplishments.* Describe how the organization has succeeded in accomplishing its goals since its inception (be brief).

6. *The Vision for the Future.* What does the organization specifically plan to accomplish (and how) in the next few years? What measures will be used to gauge the accomplishments?

7. *The Development Plan.* Present the total need (personnel, tools and money) of the organization and the time frame the need covers.

8. *Support Opportunities.* Divide the total budget into several categories—salaries, travel, overhead, publications and so on. You can also include your individual budget alongside the area, national or international budget. Also, suggest different ways to give.

9. *Agency Profile.* List some of the most pertinent characteristics of your agency or team; the number and location of staff, countries or campuses served and so on.

Regardless of the type of case used, practice it before presenting it. We spend at least half our case training time in role-play situations. Everyone who will present the personal or team case in Inter-Varsity has an opportunity to be on both sides of the presentation. Presenting to a pastor, businessperson and even members of a small group Bible study are roles we have staff practice.

As you go over the case, highlight questions that come to mind. A pastor may ask how your group helps the local church. Although that point may not be covered in the case, talk to your supervisor or a coworker about how to handle such a question. But be careful not to let questions sidetrack the presentation. In some cases it is helpful to defer questions until after you finish, or until you can get back to the questioner with a more precise answer.

Here we have talked about your support audiences and how you might describe your mission to them. You're just getting warmed up. In the next chapter we'll talk about the methods and strategy used in raising full support.

Next Steps

1. Ask your supervisor if your agency or team has ever put together a case statement. If so, obtain a copy and practice it with your coworkers. If not, suggest that you gather to write and practice one as part of your next installment of support-raising training.

2. Read the seven personal case questions and write your own ministry case statement. Practice it by role-playing with a coworker or supervisor until you are comfortable presenting it without notes.

3. Make a list of the five questions most frequently posed to your organization by pastors, businesspeople and other supporters. Have the answers approved by a supervisor before you field the questions.

7

Communication— Your Methods

So far we've covered the "software" of support raising—who to ask and what to present to different audiences. Now we come to the "hardware"—the *methods* to use in communicating support requests.

Simply addressing the how-to's of communicating a need is not enough. One must understand why various methods may or may not apply to a situation. There is no perfect or easy way to raise support. Here, as in ministry, the goal is not to be convenient or inexpensive, but to effectively communicate, understand and meet needs.

This chapter will focus on four methods for communicating support needs—letters, appointments, presentations and materials. We'll begin by discussing how to carefully choose between them.

Choosing a Channel

The local coordinator of a large mission to high-school youth bumped into one of the mission's donors at church. He asked if she had met the group's new local youth worker, Sue.

The elderly lady, smiling, said she had met the young woman twice—both times at Sue's insistence.

"Has she asked you to support her financially?" asked the

coordinator.

"No," she replied. "I think she is trying to work up the nerve to ask."

You may be at a point of doubt and anxiety about approaching the people you listed in chapter five. Most of us are uncomfortable about asking friends or family for anything, let alone money. Fear of rejection or stammering for the right words may cause us to avoid a personal presentation altogether. This feeling usually results in an apologetic *written* request for "help." You may have seen such a letter. It's the "you wouldn't want to support me, would you?" approach.

Fears and anxiety should not determine what methods we use when contacting people. Instead concentrate on the most effective method for obtaining support. Determine ahead of time a plan of action and then stick to it. Remember that God has chosen you for a tremendous opportunity, and he wants others to help. Now all you need to do is get the word out.

There are three common methods used when asking for support—face to face, by phone and in writing. Nothing is more effective than face-to-face communication. People can sense your zeal for ministry when they *see* and *hear* you express yourself. Even nervousness helps. It shows you're human and that what you have to say is important enough to warrant this talk.

A phone call is the next best method of asking for support. Today, most business is conducted over the telephone. In many instances it's even less expensive and more practical than a visit or a letter.

Letters, though, are by far the most popular. But our conclusion is that they're also the least effective. Letters can be personal, but most of the time they're not because of the size of most mailing lists and the little time we devote to writing. A letter is a good way to let everyone know of the ministry "from the field." It's also a great way to announce one's appointment. But we highly recommend you don't first ask for money in a letter unless a visit or a phone call are out of the question.

Better yet, the first request, ideally, should represent a mixture of all three methods. First a letter of introduction is sent to a prospect explaining our work and our desire to meet them face to face. In the letter we promise to contact them to set a date. Then we follow up the letter by making the call and setting the appointment. This is followed by the appointment and the request for the gift. Then we send a note of thanks and a restatement of what was discussed and agreed to.

Brochures, pamphlets and other mass-produced tools are least personal and least effective. You may choose to supplement personal contact with a preprinted budget or case statement. But they are for the most part too passive a means to use alone.

Setting Appointments

The first point to be made about appointments is to *get the appointment.* A phone call or a letter may be used to get it. Just get the appointment. We're not contradicting ourselves by discussing phone calls and letters first. Understanding the process involved in both is important in order to set up face-to-face meetings with people.

Four points come into play before calling or writing to set up an appointment to request support.

First, the organization or team must have a plan from which all personal goals stem—a broader case statement which cites the mission of the organization (see the team case outline on pp. 48-49).

Second is the personal case statement that stems from the mission of the organization. For example, "XYZ agency's goal is to present Jesus Christ to Central America, using radio in a variety of ways. I will be doing technical repair on equipment at two stations." (See the personal case example on pp. 46-47.)

Third, have a list of prospects. Whether working through your original list of supporters or five referred businesspeople, be sure to know who and where they are. To contact either the wrong person or the right person at the wrong time is embarrassing.

Finally, having a great desire to set up appointments is important.

In just beginning to raise support that may mean a sentence or two in an initial letter to request an appointment. Try something like, "I plan to call you next week to set a time to discuss my support need and how you can help." Sending a note in advance of calling is always a good idea. Let them know who you are and what you're asking of them. And then be sure to call at the appointed time.

Using the Phone

Jody, who was raising support for a high-school mission, was calling the mother of a friend to borrow a household item. She had also sent the family a letter requesting support a few weeks earlier. Before Jody could say why she had called, the mother apologized profusely for forgetting to send a gift. She promised to get it in the mail *immediately*.

What would have happened if she hadn't called?

Another missionary on deputation had an appointment with a pastor scheduled weeks in advance. When Phil arrived at the appointed time (or so he thought), the pastor wasn't there. The appointment was an hour earlier. The missionary neglected to call to confirm their meeting.

The telephone *must* become a major tool in support raising for a number of reasons. First, the phone is convenient, economical and effective. Second, many more people can be contacted by phone than face-to-face visits in the same time period. Third, referrals can be followed up more quickly and economically. And finally, not only will the phone improve productivity, but it also cuts down on interruptions which may occur in face-to-face presentations.

But not everyone enjoys using the telephone. For some there is a fear in calling because of possible rejection. For others, the fear is rooted either in calling people they don't know or in not knowing enough about their job in order to speak clearly about it.

Support raising is largely a mental and emotional activity. Using the following steps may help you overcome any phoning fears you may have: (1) Identify the cause of the fear so you can pray for a calm yet bold spirit. (2) Know as much as possible about where the person you're calling stands in relationship to your ministry. (3) Prepare to describe yourself and your work succinctly. (4) Listen carefully to their comments and questions. Answer questions clearly. If you don't have an answer, say so, and tell the person you'll get back to them when you do. (5) Be positive when you call. Never apologize for calling. (6) Remember that the worst thing the person can say is no. They're not rejecting you—*no* doesn't mean "never." You are calling to find out where they stand in supporting you.

Here is a sample phone conversation to use as a guide. Though this example is based on someone contacting a new, potential supporter, most of the techniques are the same for any situation.

1. Hello Mr./Mrs. _____, this is Cindy Johnson. I'm calling to follow up on the letter I sent you about my work with SEND International. Were you able to read it?

2. How familiar are you with our ministry? Do you have any questions about SEND, or the work I'm doing? (Be prepared with answers.)

3. (At this point, you may wish to set up an appointment to talk face to face about support, rather than over the phone. If this is not possible, then bring up the question of support now.) I wanted to get back to you to see if you'd like to support me. Will you be able to support me (us) this year? (Stop talking—wait for an answer.)

4. (If the answer is yes . . .) Thank you very much for your commitment. I'll be writing to keep you informed of my prayer needs and the progress we're making with SEND. (You may want to explain *how* the person should go about sending in their gift.)

(If the answer is no, or not now . . .) Would you like to receive my newsletter to keep you informed of the ministry? Perhaps you would like me to contact you again in a few months? I will appreciate your prayers and encouragement. Thank you!

When calling someone, first identify who you are and why you are calling. Ask them if they have received your letter. See if they have any general questions about the organization and if they would be interested in meeting. Let the person you're calling determine when to meet. The time of the appointment will depend on whether you're calling a businessperson or someone who would like his or her spouse present. Unless you're hosting a small dessert or presentation, ask to meet in their home. People are most comfortable in their home environment.

If calling to ask for support, see if they are interested in hearing about the mission. Follow the general outline of the case statements; condense the information and make it sound conversational. No one likes to be read to. Ask what aspects of the ministry they are interested in hearing more about.

At some point you can ask if they are interested in supporting you. Give them time to answer. You may want to call twice—once to present your ministry and need, and again to ask for an answer. This gives them time to think and pray. If the answer is yes, thank them, tell them how they are to send their gift and let them know you will keep them informed about prayer needs and the progress of the ministry. If no, ask them why not, or if they still would like to receive your prayer letters or if they would like to be contacted again in a couple months. Even if they are not interested in supporting you regularly, they may be open to giving a special, one-time gift—especially if you have identified a particular need, like a conference, which they could help you with. With either answer, be sure to be positive and thank them for their time and interest.

A call that results in a good conversation should be acknowledged within two days. Send a personal note of thanks or meeting reminder along with printed information about the agency's work.

Appointments and Presentations
We've used personal presentations as the example when setting up an appointment. This is between you and one or two others, preferably in their home or over a meal at a restaurant. Another

situation is with a small group. This could be a dessert hosted by you or at a Bible study meeting. You may also be asked to present your ministry before a large church congregation or an organization's monthly meeting (for example, the Kiwanis). Though there are differences in the way to present yourself before various sized groups, we'll focus on aspects of the presentation that should remain constant, no matter what group is being addressed.

1. At the outset let us *emphasize prayer*. Pray for those whom you'll meet, for yourself, for your presentation and for God to be honored by your meeting.

2. *Dress appropriately*—preferably at the "high end" of your audience. In other words, don't alienate the group or individual by what you wear, whether slacks, a suit or a dress. Never wear jeans. What you wear often communicates how you feel about your hosts. This is very important because many of us size a person up by appearance—even before the presentation begins. Be complementary in appearance.

3. *Set your appointment or presentation well in advance,* so proper planning can take place. Don't let yourself get put on a meeting agenda with four other special announcements. Insist on a time when you'll be the sole presenter.

4. *Develop a checklist* of items to be done in advance. Do you need to order more brochures from your agency's office? Do you need to check the media show in advance to make sure it works properly? Do you need to make a restaurant reservation? And will you pay for the dinner?

5. *Practice the presentation* before a spouse or a friend. Time yourself so you can cut the talk to fit the allotted time. Practice answering a few questions as well.

6. When meeting in a person's home, *arrive just on time.* Surprising your hosts in the midst of cleaning up after a meal is not a good start. Arrive five to ten minutes early for a meeting with a businessperson or a pastor. Use the extra time to check your appearance, relax and locate either the person you're meeting or his or her secretary.

7. *The initiative belongs to the people you are visiting.* Let them seat you, initiate small talk and ask you about your purpose in coming. Maintain good posture, eye contact and a confident voice. Pace yourself so as not to rush, but keep an eye on the clock. Follow the outline you rehearsed, but pause occasionally to make sure you're being understood. Even if the conversation is very warm and comfortable, don't let the relaxed atmosphere allow you to go overtime. People appreciate your commitment to brevity. Take cues from your host. If he or she asks you not to rush off, then stay a bit longer.

Good preparation shows up quickly in the conversation. Eye contact will be easier, and you'll pick up verbal and nonverbal cues in order to pace your message and listen attentively—rather than fret over what to say next.

8. At the close of the presentation, summarize your points and *request support.* "Mr. Jones, given the opportunity I've described, would you support my [our] work this year?" Personability and eye contact don't mean as much if people aren't asked for a decision. If they need time to think and pray, tell them you will call or visit again. Do not let them call you back unless there is total resistance to your taking the initiative. People can forget and leave you hanging too easily.

Express thanks for the time given to you, and the interest expressed in the mission. Reiterate your plan to follow up, then leave.

9. After the appointment, *follow up* according to your agreement. If the decision won't be made within a week, send an immediate note of thanks, along with any requested materials. Otherwise, simply include words of appreciation for time together when you call.

10. Finally, *record pertinent information* of the contact (date, location, information requested) for future reference. Use the Support Record sheet (figure 5.1) for this purpose. Even if the person responds negatively, you can always return later with another request. A return visit will be easier if the reason for the initial acceptance or rejection is recorded.

Writing Letters

Why are you writing? Are you writing to *inform,* or to *request* something in return? Informative letters can serve a variety of purposes. The authors of the books of the Bible wrote to teach, encourage, thank and exhort. Your prayer letters (written regularly while you're in ministry) can play a similar role with your supporters. This is discussed at greater length in chapter ten.

Here we're speaking of letters used to request support. Someone out of reach of a visit deserves a personal letter explaining your mission and opportunities to support. But while a written request may be something to fall back on, we discourage using it as an initial request for support. It is a passive medium—one which asks the reader to respond without benefit of personal contact.

Before writing the letter, determine the basic purpose of the correspondence. Don't confuse the reader by cluttering up the letter with personal notes, ministry news, prayer requests and a request for support. Potential supporters will not process so many items. Sit down and outline the content of the letter. The following are five guidelines to get you started.

1. Determine what three important things you want the reader to remember. More items will only confuse them.

2. Determine what your most important point is. Remember that this letter is *for supporters.* Consider what is important and interesting for them regarding your work.

3. Try to make this point in an effective and interesting way. Notice which elements of a newspaper or magazine draw you to them. Most people are attracted to real stories about real people. Graphics or photos also help catch readers' attention. Experiment with different methods to make your points stand out.

4. Give enough background information to allow the supporters to understand and empathize. Stay away from shop talk— abbreviations, acronyms and coined evangelical phrases. This also involves reader sensitivity. We can't assume readers have as great an understanding of the organization or mission field as we do. This is difficult, especially when we write many reports or have reg-

ular dialog with coworkers. We easily become stale and withdrawn from the outside world. Emphasize experiences, feelings, outcomes and their value.

5. After writing the letter, put it aside for a day or two, and then read it again to see if the points are made in an interesting way. The best test for successful writing is whether or not *you* would voluntarily read the letter. Also, have a friend read it and critique it. If the letter fails to flow smoothly or is unclear, start the process over. The point is *not* just to kick out a letter. Nor are you to produce a masterpiece. The goal is simply for readers to easily read and understand what is said. Few will read the entire letter—and fewer still will remember its content—if it isn't interesting. See the sample letters at the end of the chapter (figures 7.1 and 7.2).

Remember to be personal. Be sure to sign the first letter to parents and close friends. Speak in terms of *you* and *me*. Though you are writing to a group, they won't read it as a group. Addressing the first draft to a representative from the group—Dear Jean—will help to avoid generalizations in your writing.

Typewritten letters look more official, while handwritten letters seem more personal. Depending on the content of the letter, determine which would be more appropriate. For example, a letter about your feelings regarding nursing in India may best be handwritten, rather than typed. But have a friend lovingly comment on your handwriting before trying this.

Use shorter sentences and paragraphs to make the letter readable. Choose ink and paper color that doesn't tax the readers' eyes. For example, stay away from dark green ink on light green paper. Black ink on white, earth tones, or pastel paper is best. Be sensitive to the overall look of the letter. Do words run from one edge to the other? Leave at least a one-inch margin all around. Is the ink dark enough for good reproduction? Date the letter for the day you plan to mail it. A letter dated Spring 1984 doesn't mean much when it's mailed in July. People who receive the letter will check for several things—correct spelling of their name, stamped postage, the date at the top of the letter, a salutation and a

June 21, 1984

Dear Jack and Diane,

I would like to share with you an exciting opportunity that God has opened up for us. I have been accepted to work with Inner-City Impact! Inner-City Impact is an interdenominational ministry seeking to reach and serve the people of our nation's cities. Debbie and I are convinced that the city is a crucial place to be. We look around us and see how many people are living in major metropolitan areas and we know God wants us with Inner-City.

We ourselves have been in New York for the past twenty years!

We're writing because we consider you two to be among our dearest friends. And right now we're in the process of talking to friends and family about becoming involved in our ministry through regular support.

Debbie and I would like to get together with you sometime in the coming few weeks to talk further about our upcoming ministry. While we have been accepted on staff with Inner-City, we cannot officially begin work until $1,500 a month in support is raised. This includes costs for salary, training, insurance and office expenses. Right now we're seeking 60 partners to help us with gifts of $25 per month.

In addition, to have an effective outreach to the city, we know we need strong prayer support. We need friends who will share in our struggles through their committed prayer.

Please read the enclosed brochure which describes Inner-City Impact. The work it outlines is similar to what we will be doing where we live. We want to answer your questions and describe the work in more detail when we get together.

Talk over the possibilities for meeting with us. And pray for us as we seek supporters. We really want to get together with you two in person soon. One of us will call within the coming week to set up a time.

We're excited! We hope you can be too, along with us. May God bless you richly through His loving provision.

In Him,

John and Debbie Schmidt

Figure 7.1   Sample letter for friends (or with slight modification for family)

September 6, 1984

Dear Angie,

I'm writing to let you know about a project that many of us at Inter-Varsity are working on. Before I ask for your help, let me share a little bit of background.

Over two and a half years ago, I was offered a position with Inter-Varsity's Income Department in Madison, Wisconsin. I believe the Lord opened that door for me—at just the right time in my life. Now I am privileged to share in Inter-Varsity's important ministry of reaching college students for Jesus Christ.

The IVCF Income Department consists of seven staff responsible for processing gifts of about fifteen million dollars annually. We assist Inter-Varsity's campus ministry by providing vital financial information to our staff. We also promptly receipt over fifteen thousand donors each month. We're "behind the scenes," exercising the gift of administration (1 Cor 12:27-28) necessary for Inter-Varsity's work to continue.

What do I gain from this work? First, I am privileged to lead a team of committed, responsible and productive people. They've also taught *me* a lot over the past two and a half years. I have been challenged, encouraged and often humbled by their godly example. And second, I often see the results of the campus work we help make possible. This spring, Cindy and I assisted with a Seniors Appreciation Banquet for the University of Wisconsin Inter-Varsity chapter, emphasizing again the importance of a vital campus fellowship.

How can you get involved? First, pray for me. I do need God's strength and guidance as I set goals, schedule priorities, correspond with our supporters and simply work closely with others. Second, you can help by giving financially to my work with Inter-Varsity. I have a monthly support goal of $500.00 for the next twelve months.

Will you help us raise this support for the coming year? Your gift of $15, $20 or $25 each month will go a long way toward continuing this essential administrative ministry. You can give and pray toward my goal, as God leads you. Please use the enclosed envelope if you wish to pledge or give now.

Thanks for your consideration—it means a lot to us!
Sincerely,

David and Cindy Patterson

P.S.   I've enclosed a brochure which may help explain Inter-Varsity's work more completely. Cindy and I are looking forward to having you on our support team!

Figure 7.2   Sample letter for acquaintances or referrals

postscript (P.S.). Though the P.S. was originally intended for notes one forgot to include in the letter, it can be used to remind the reader of an important point. Effectiveness of a P.S. is diminished, though, when overused.

Check the letter carefully for typos, misspellings and awkward sentences before having it printed. Many people will notice misspelled words and take them as an indication of the way you do ministry (hurriedly).

Talk to a supervisor or coworker when it comes time to print the letter. A certain amount of time must be allowed for printing and mailing by the date on the letter. Printing is recommended when the letter has photos or special graphic designs included. If the mailing list is large enough, offset printing may be less expensive than photocopying.

If the domestic United States mailing list numbers over two hundred, check into getting a bulk permit. Ask your supervisor what mailing (postage) options are available. If overseas, always use airmail—even if it means writing less frequently. Surface rate takes up to a month to deliver—if at all. And for all special letters (announcements or emergency appeals), use first-class rates. Keep a supply of commemorative stamps on hand for such occasions. They will help distinguish your letters from the crowd.

Earlier we mentioned asking for support, or some sort of response, in a letter. This can be done when a visit or phone call just isn't possible. If something is requested from the reader, enclose a convenient means for them to respond. A business reply envelope with designation for support should accompany all financial requests (see figure 7.3). Include a self-addressed, stamped, preprinted postcard for written replies (prayer or mailing list requests).

Using Brochures
We noted earlier that, while not being the most effective means of communication, brochures can be effective as a supplement to letters or personal presentations.

Name (Mr., Ms., Rev.)   Inter-Varsity Donor ID Number (if known)

Address   City   State   Zip

Please send information about **Inter-Varsity** to:

Name (Mr., Ms., Rev.)

Address   City   State   Zip

I want to share in the ministry of Inter-Varsity by my tax deductible gift of:

☐ $500   ☐ $100   ☐ $50   ☐ $25   ☐ $_____

Please use my gift for:

$_____ The work of staff member _____

$_____ Where it's needed most

$_____ Other _____

Please make your check or money order payable to **Inter-Varsity Christian Fellowship.**

"You will be enriched in every way for great generosity, which through us will produce thanksgiving to God."
                                                                    2 Corinthians 9:11

BUSINESS REPLY CARD
FIRST CLASS   PERMIT NO. 2259   MADISON, WI

POSTAGE WILL BE PAID BY ADDRESSEE

Inter-Varsity Christian Fellowship
233 Langdon Street
Madison, Wisconsin 53791

NO POSTAGE
NECESSARY
IF MAILED
IN THE
UNITED STATES

Figure 7.3   The sender's name, address and other pertinent information is requested on the inside of a Business Reply Envelope (BRE). The front of all BREs (bottom) displays the return address, bulk permit number and bar code.

Recently, Inter-Varsity produced a brochure that answered questions our supporters most frequently ask. Before this, many personal and standardized letters were written to respond to these questions. A lot of time was saved by using the brochure. Similar approaches have been taken with special audiences like parents, residents of Florida and potential Christian workers. Individual needs and interests are often addressed more accurately and less expensively with the help of a brochure, prayer card, map or leaflet.

The same procedure for developing a personal case statement (pp. 46-47) can be applied to produce a brochure. For example, a brochure can be a succinct, inexpensive means of publicizing yourself at several church presentations. Consider what is most important for the congregation to know: your calling, a bit of background, where you'll be, what you'll be doing, what you need and how they can help. Include a photograph of yourself. Also include a simple means for them to respond, such as the back panel of the brochure. Have the brochure edited and talk to a printer about having it typeset and produced. Strike a balance between an inexpensive brochure and a cheap-looking one. Printing that looks expensive probably isn't when you consider the importance of readability and duration. Consider the maximum number you'll need, then print ten to twenty per cent more. It's less expensive to print one larger order than several smaller ones. We've been surprised how quickly brochures are used.

Response cards are essential elements to any presentation when seeking something in return. Letters can include return envelopes and/or a response card for personal reply. A talk is usually punctuated with handing out these or a brochure containing a response panel.

Including a business reply envelope (BRE) with every mailing has become second nature for organizations (see figure 7.3). To the recipient it's a free means of sending a gift or to request information. To the organization, the BRE assures proper delivery and, in some cases, a more accurate designation of the gift it contains.

Last is our miscellaneous materials category. Some items that might be included in a mailing to supporters are a monthly prayer calendar, a budget page (see figure 4.1) and a small map of the area of mission. The budget page is an essential supplement for first meetings with churches and organizations. Besides the basic budget and need, it should contain a breakdown and explanation of how administrative money is used. Most overseas missionaries produce a map of their country or province, pinpointing their location, areas/cities they work in and vital statistics on the people they work with.

Church bulletin inserts are widely used to supplement a talk given before a congregation. They can effectively address church concerns that relate to your work on one side and address how you're meeting them on the other. Always include some means of response on the insert itself (coupon and/or name and address). See the sample in chapter eight, figure 8.3.

Personalized Christmas and thank-you cards for supporters are also possibilities. Though they aren't intended to ask for anything, cards can be gentle reminders to continue a support relationship.

Next Steps
1. Using the case statement you put together in chapter six, outline a letter of introduction to your relatives.

2. Using the same case, write your own sample phone conversation to set up a meeting with relatives living in your city. For example, you may ask one of them to hold a dessert for you; then you do the inviting over the phone.

3. Outline the talk you will give asking your relatives for support. Practice it with your spouse or with one of your family members. Rehearse and edit it to say what you want said in a given time period.

8

Support
from Churches

Churches are the backbone of missionary support. Agencies and individuals must build strong ties with local churches in order to be most effective in ministry. All stand to benefit from a close support relationship between churches and Christian workers.

Churches are collections of individuals with resources we need—prayers, finances and encouragement. Most of these resources are at the disposal of one or a few individuals in charge of disbursing them on behalf of the church. The congregation, in turn, may need access to our ministry gifts and audience. If Marc is working in prison ministry, and the church isn't involved in that ministry (but wants to be), he may be just the person they're looking for to support. Still others may want to be involved because of the nature or location of the mission work.

We know of a few churches who send people from their congregation into mission work fully supported. There are those who firmly believe the church is responsible to cover all or most of a member's ministry expense. But the more typical example is the church that in smaller ways supports many projects. Missionaries sent from their midst don't often receive more than a few hundred dollars per month.

Some people are reluctant to approach a church to ask for

support. As one friend put it, "How can I expect support from a church when I can offer them little time in return?" The question is one of balance, really. We *can* provide ministry resources to the congregation—even if we're not available to teach them. In the case of student work, a campus staff worker can encourage students to attend the churches, while at the same time offering campus fellowship and training to students already in the church. In the case of overseas missionaries, they can offer guidance on missions for interested members of the congregation. So while support may be an initial goal, it need not be the only one. Mutual involvement will grow from support.

Before beginning to make church contacts, it's important to understand the process involved. An old business maxim is that eighty per cent of the business will come from twenty per cent of the customers. The eighty-twenty rule also applies to church support raising. We mean that eighty per cent of the results (or support) will tend to come from twenty per cent of the contacts. Of course, this is just an average. But being concerned about time management, we should not focus equal attention to all of our support contacts. Identify which twenty per cent of the contacts are capable of providing eighty per cent of the support goal. They are the people to work with. In most cases this group includes churches that can focus people's support on you. The other eighty per cent of the supporters should take twenty per cent of your support-raising efforts so your time is maximized.

This concept is important to church support for two reasons. First, it changes our focus. We will have greater discernment with church and individual contacts. We can try to determine if a contact will bring an eighty-per-cent return or a twenty-per-cent return, and act accordingly.

Second, the rule will change our expectations. For instance, a tire salesperson can sell some tires to individuals and several to gas stations. But he'll have to make many contacts and sales to keep a healthy pace. What if he went to a General Motors assembly plant? He can ask them to buy his tires, but chances are they won't on the first, or even the second, visit. He will have to spend a lot of time getting their account. But once he has it, he'll probably sell half a million tires in one day. The salesperson had greater expectations approaching the plant and went away with great results.

This helps us understand the church. Not all are on a scale of a GM plant. But there are greater resources involved in a church than with an individual. Repeated contacts are needed with the church, but the expectations for support are greater.

Basically there are three divisions to church support raising: initial contacts, the appointment and follow-up.

Initial Contacts

An exercise in chapter nine will ask you to list the churches and pastors you know you can contact for support. You need to keep several points in mind as you do this. First, make the list as long as possible. Think not only of your home and current churches, but also those of your parents, relatives and friends. At this point you can't be sure if those churches will be interested. Talk to other supporters to get an introduction to their churches. Put the churches on your list.

If you are unfamiliar with a church, talk to a friend in the church, read their monthly newsletter and get a copy of their annual financial statement to discover what the church's interests are. If you're part of a multiministry organization, try using another focus to get into the church. They may be interested in radio broadcasts or literature distribution or some other aspect of your overall mission. Talk to the pastor too to find out who is interested in what particular fields.

Schedule time for church contacts. Churches are long-term support projects. Most take at least a year to write you into their budget. And budgeting times vary with denominations. What this means is that key churches should be contacted right away. If you've just arrived in a new city, call each local pastor as soon as possible. Ask for an appointment to present your work to the pastor or the missions committee chairperson or both. If you wait months to call, your hesitancy may come back to haunt you.

Find out at what time of year the church puts together its budget. Most compile theirs in the fall. Consequently, you must get your request to the proper officers as soon as possible. If you don't get to the church until spring or winter, use the months that follow to meet members of the congregation. Prepare for next year's request. And look into the possibility of receiving a special midyear or end-of-year gift. Sometimes churches will have special or leftover funds for such requests.

One church had a man visit from Mission Aviation Fellowship (MAF) at missions conference time. The church only wanted a booth and some MAF materials. The MAF representative wanted to be there to answer questions. The pastor was reluctant because he didn't want the man to ask people for funds. He promised he wouldn't do any fundraising. He didn't pass out any prayer cards. He just stood by his booth and answered questions. The pastor was impressed that the MAF man did just what he said he would do.

That was in February. In June he was on the budget. Why? He built relationships by talking to everyone who stopped at his booth.

Church members asked the pastor, "Do you know that young man is going to Africa?"

"Yes."

"Do you know that he needs support?"

"Yes."

"Well, what are we going to do about it?"

The congregation applied pressure to get him on their budget. The church is now covering thirty per cent of his support.

Have an agenda in mind when you call. Be prepared to be flexible in *how* you cover your points, being sensitive to the situation. In other words, try to get to know the pastors and their concerns in ministry. How much do they know about the agency's ministry? How long have they been in the community? Has the congregation already expressed an interest in your area of work?

What special emphasis are they developing in the church (such as relationships, social concerns, evangelism or missions)? Let them get to know you personally.

Here's a sample agenda from Gail, an Inter-Varsity staff member who was trying to raise additional support because of increased costs. You can adapt it to your own mission situation:

a. I am seeking to develop good working relationships with local churches. I want to discover how we can help and complement one another in ministry.

b. Here is the current situation in IVCF . . . (emphasizing locations of chapters and staff, and the major emphases in our ministry if the pastor is not very familiar with IVCF).

c. We'd like to help you minister to your college students. If you'd care to send me names and addresses of students from your church, I'd be happy to have the appropriate chapter contact them.

d. Are there other ways we can help you? (You may offer to speak to groups at this church, or to conduct workshops or conferences—but only on a limited basis. Don't overcommit yourself to the neglect of your own work. Do not commit yourself to anything immediately. Ask for time to review your calendar, offering to let the pastor know within a couple of days.)

e. I also need support. First, for people to pray regularly for my work. I also need to raise $5,000 in this state in order to stay on campus. Can you help me raise this money by putting Inter-Varsity in your missions budget? If not, then can you help us by allowing us to share with your people what I am doing, in the hope that some of them might want to support my mission? (One pastor sought an invitation for the staff person to speak about Inter-Varsity to his older adults group. He said they were the most affluent group in his church and would be the most likely to give!)

f. I would be happy to come back again sometime to meet with a missions committee, or to speak at a service. We also have a slide and sound presentation which I could bring along to help explain our ministry. Also, is there someone else I should speak to at this time? Perhaps the missions committee chairperson?

g. Here is a brochure about Inter-Varsity for you and your missions committee. (You might also want to leave a gift book for the pastor.)

h. Here is my card, so that you know how to reach me. If you are going to discuss this with your missions committee, shall I call you (get a specific day), or should I wait to hear from you?

i. Thank you.

The five churches Gail visited were all Presbyterian. She heard from four out of the five pastors that their people were not happy with the procedure of giving their missions funds to the denomination for disbursement. Instead, they chose to designate all their missions giving personally. These particular congregations tended to be more open to donating to interdenominational groups, if they were convinced it was a worthwhile cause. As we mentioned, an agenda is just a list of the major points you want to get across. One's approach should vary with each church, depending on its style of missions support. Take some time to discover what that style is.

Some appointments will be made by phone. But we've also included a few sample letters of introduction to churches outside of your city. Figure 8.1 is a sample letter to a pastor. Figure 8.2 is a similar introduction to a church missions committee. In either case, if you have a friend in the church, use his or her name in the letter. You may even ask your friend to write the introductory letter (or call) for you. The same is true if you discover any alumni of your work in the church. Their endorsement can be a great asset—especially in an unfamiliar church.

It will also help to get a copy of the church budget. Most churches provide one. From it, you can see if or how much they support your area of mission work. If you recognize the name of one of their missionaries, give the person a call. Ask him or her what procedure was followed to obtain support. You may also

May 21, 1984

Dear Pastor Huston,

China is a vast mission field of about one billion people. There are people of different ethnic backgrounds, occupations and interests. This is the mission field I feel the Lord is calling me to as a teacher of English as a second language.

I want to share Jesus Christ with the millions of Chinese who have never heard one clear word of the gospel. World Evangelical Fellowship, of Wheaton, Illinois, has provided the method and the organization for me to go.

I am appealing to the missions committee of First Church to consider me as a missionary candidate to Shanghai, China. Only as provision is made can I go and minister as a teacher and follower of Christ.

I am seeking a pledge of $100 per month from your missions committee. My budget is $1,500 per month, or $18,000 a year. This includes salary, travel and administration for my service overseas.

Would you and the members of your missions committee be able to meet with me to discuss my mission and need?

My desire is to be given the opportunity to minister to people in your congregation through their involvement in my work. It would be a pleasure to speak to the congregation to explain my calling and plans for service.

I will call you early next week to set a time for us to meet.

May God bless you at First Church as you seek to bring glory and honor to our Lord.

In Christ,

Beth Taylor
1234 James St.
Chicago, Illinois 60187
555-0039

Figure 8.1   A sample letter to a pastor requesting a hearing before the missions committee

Mrs. Mary Swanson   May 31, 1984
Chairperson, Missions Committee
Bethel Presbyterian Church
Norfolk, Virginia

Dear Mrs. Swanson:

On the advice of the pastor I am sending a formal request to the missions committee to consider including International Students Incorporated (ISI) in the 1985 missions budget in the church.

So that you may have information concerning our work, I am enclosing a brochure that fully explains who we are and what we do.

I also feel you should know more about me personally. I was saved early in life, but never really acknowledged the lordship of Christ until I was brought face to face with issues during my college days. Through the ministry of ISI, and a relationship with staff persons who visited our campus, I was brought to a place of complete commitment to Jesus Christ. Only this past year did I feel called to become a full-time minister of Christ—called to declare Jesus Christ to international students on American college campuses. Since then, my time has been spent in preparation for ministry.

For me to minister on Norfolk campuses as an ISI staff member, I need to raise a total budget of $15,000. This budget includes all expenses incurred in my travel, training, and administration. There are no hidden or later costs.

Will the missions committee consider helping me by placing me in the missions budget for $500 a year?

In order to help you consider me as one of your missionaries, I would like to have a part in your next missions conference. It would be my purpose to come to the church at regular intervals and report to you and the congregation on what God is doing among international students in Norfolk. I will also be available to speak to your high school and college students. I want to offer your church many resources. We can also minister to your students who are away at schools in distant places, where we have staff.

If you'd like more information, I'll be happy to come and address your committee. May God continue to give guidance and blessings to you and your congregation.

Sincerely in Him,

Bill Lanza
416 Highfield
Royal Oak, Michigan 40187

Figure 8.2   Letter to missions committee chairperson

discover who the decision-maker is for church giving.

The Appointment
The next step is an appointment with the pastor or missions committee. Dress neatly for the meeting. Be sure any media presentations are in working order before you arrive. If you're meeting a group, bring enough material for each person to have copies. Put your name, address and phone number on everything you hand out. (Review the agenda outline on pages 57-58).

You don't need to overimpress your hosts with a formal presentation. You're among partners in ministry—be yourself. Back up goals and claims of the ministry with stories of real people—preferably those you or your predecessor have helped in ministry. And be prepared for hard questions. "What do you hope to accomplish while overseas?" "What does your work have to do with *our* church?" "What percentage of your budget goes toward administration?" And be careful what you say. Share the agency's purposes, but stay away from discussions over theological differences. That's not the purpose of the meeting.

Don't understate the importance of your work. The advantages of face-to-face meetings are eye contact, gestures and the enthusiasm in your voice. Project the excitement you feel for your mission.

Some missionaries have a hard time knowing what to ask of a church. Two Christian workers had an appointment with a pastor, presented their inner-city work to him, stated financial needs and set up a date to make a presentation to the church. A month later they spoke at the evening service. The pastor announced that the members would have an opportunity to share through a faith-promise offering. When the two finished speaking, the ushers collected the gifts and pledges. The forty-two people present pledged a total of $150—a *month*!

So how much should *you* ask for? We've found that if a pastor or missions committee asks how much others give, the best response is to start at the top. If you say, "Some give $10 or more . . . ," the church will give $10. If you say, "Some give $2,000, others give less," the church will think of what they can do, not what others do. Our best advice, given the church budget, is to suggest a few levels of giving and then leave it to God and the church to decide.

Before you thank the pastor and leave, ask him for the names of other area pastors to contact. We know of one Methodist pastor who, when asked for a referral, volunteered to send a letter of endorsement to every Methodist church in his New England district.

Follow-up

The final step of church support raising comes after the appointment. Send a personal letter thanking each person for his or her time. Repeat what was discussed or decided. You may want to send a book to the pastor as a token of appreciation—even if no support was pledged. Keep a file card or record sheet on each church contacted (see p. 37). Write notes on what was talked about and what their response was. List materials you gave or promised them.

You may be invited back to address the congregation. If time allows, bring something to show them (a media show or map). And ask if inserts may be placed in the church bulletins on the day you'll be speaking. Prepare one that supplements your talk. Be sure it repeats basic information about the ministry, your name and address, and the opportunity to respond. The sample shown in Figure 8.3 has a response panel to indicate a person's interest.

Transferring support from you to your replacement is one thing few do well. If your name is on a church budget, and you're planning to end your mission in June, you may still be scheduled to receive money through the end of the year. Talk to the pastor about transferring the support to your replacement (if there is one). Let him know she'll be doing the same work in the same place— just as you did. Give him or the church treasurer specific instructions to change the designation of their gift.

Keep in mind that there are no quick returns from church

Inter-Varsity Christian Fellowship

Our Mission is Students . . .

Students take the lead in forming and directing their own Inter-Varsity chapters. Staff workers, trained and commissioned by Inter-Varsity, are sent to motivate students, enlarge their Christian vision, guide, and encourage. Through small group Bible studies, personal counseling and group activities, they . . .

- *Disciple* young Christians and assist them in growing in their faith.
- Teach and model a lifestyle of *evangelism*.
- Stimulate interest and participation in *world missions*.

Our Work is an Extension of the Church . . .

Some young people go away to college and lose track of their home church. Our staff are often able to encourage their church involvement while they're in school. Many churches support local staff members as missionaries to the university community. Staff are involved as leaders in a variety of denominations as well. As a result, thousands of pastors and lay leaders are serving churches today because of Inter-Varsity's impact on their lives.

We're on Campuses Near You . . .

Inter-Varsity now serves on more campuses than any other Christian organization. Our wide range of ministries includes Inter-Varsity Press, Nurses Christian Fellowship, Ethnic Ministries, the Urbana Student Missions Convention, and more.

Will you help us reach students for Jesus Christ? Please fill out the attached form and return it to:

I want to help reach students for Jesus Christ!

☐ Through regular prayer—send me your newsletter.
☐ Through my gift of ☐ $25 ☐ $30 ☐ Other $ _____
☐ I'd like more information. Please contact me at:

Name _____ Phone _____

Address _____ City _____ State ____ Zip _____

Inter-Varsity Christian Fellowship, 233 Langdon, Madison, WI 53703, (608) 257-0263

Figure 8.3   This church bulletin insert was inexpensively produced and given to everyone attending a Sunday evening service. Distributing general information in writing enables the speaker to concentrate on personal testimony and needs.

contacts. Each has its own resources and procedures that you need to fit into. Continue regular contact, whether they support you or not. Be persistent. Once a church agrees to support you, they usually do so indefinitely.

Next Steps
1. Compose a letter to your home pastor, announcing your appointment to your agency.

2. Call your pastor to set up a time to meet to discuss how the church might support you. Follow the process through to the point of asking either the pastor or the missions committee (whoever makes allocations) to make a pledge.

9

The Support Plan

We now have all the elements needed to plan support contacts. In chapter five we talked about listing and segmenting potential supporters. Later we dealt with understanding the interests of these segments and how to communicate our support needs to them. The next step is to draw these things together into strategies and an overall plan.

Why a strategy? People keep busy schedules. Also, many people need to be contacted to get full support, often as many as two hundred. Churches require even more time and effort before they'll consider a support request. Planning is essential.

Most important, for many the whole idea of support raising is intimidating. Many of us look at the task and think, "I'll never raise all my support. I need too much money, and there's too much to do between now and the time I'm supposed to be on the field." The task becomes so big in our minds we shrink from it. We either do too little too late, or too much without a plan and never reach our goal.

Having a plan helps to prevent these problems. Each step is written down with the time frame to do it in. Begin by developing a strategy to contact different groups of potential supporters. Take it in steps, following a timetable. Leave room for evaluation and have a Plan B, in case you don't obtain all the pledged support you need. The amount of detail in this process depends on you. The goal is not to contact as many people as possible, nor is it to send out all the information available on your ministry. The goal is to raise the support needed to get and keep you on the mission field. In this chapter we'll outline the process for support planning.

The Strategies

A strategy is to a plan what a chapter is to a book. It is a short series of steps taken with one segment of the support list. Eventually for each group on the list there will be a strategy for reaching them with your support needs. Begin with your closest friends. By now you should have some idea what you want to communicate to them about your upcoming mission. How will you go about it? We suggest three basic steps.

First, send a personally addressed letter of introduction to each one. The version may be the same as what you plan to send to other segments of your list. State the facts (case), including your desire to get together personally to talk about support. Remember, these are your friends, so don't be too formal. Tell each of them you want to set a time to meet. You may want to do this individually or at a reception with the whole group. Say you will call to set it up.

Second, call each person to set a time *as soon as possible.*

Third, get together to make your presentation. Ask for support. If they want to think or pray about the decision, tell them you'll call to get an answer. *Thank them.*

Call back in a week or so if your friend hasn't already gotten back to you with an answer.

Simple. Now continue in the same vein with members of your family. For those relatives too far away to visit, close your introductory letter by asking for specific support help: "Uncle Bill, I'm asking everyone in the family to help me with $15 a month in support. Will you help me in my ministry? I've enclosed an envelope and a card for you to fill out and return by the end of the month. I'll call you next week to see if you've made a decision or if you have questions."

Plan to call within a week after they receive the letter. And when you call—relax. Simply ask Uncle Bill if he received and read your letter. "Any questions? Can I count on your support this year?" Sometimes familiarity makes it hard to ask family and friends for money. But you ultimately need an answer in order to know where you stand. Give Uncle Bill adequate time to decide. Then help him, and you, by asking for an answer.

Not all out-of-town contacts need to begin and end with a letter. Ask your supervisor for funds to visit other towns where friends and family are concentrated. Save time by setting up appointments before you leave home. Or find out if your agency's office or a business friend has MCI or a WATS line you can use. Use the money you'll save to call more people.

The Plan

Once you've devised a strategy for each audience, pull them all together into a plan. With the help of many missionaries we've developed a planning format for support raising. It is designed to help you establish goals and combine various steps into a timetable. One thing to keep in mind as you begin—aim to contact and ask for more than you may actually need to meet your support goal. How much is enough? That's most easily answered by saying you should contact as many people as possible, and ask for as much support as they can or want to give. Beyond that, Christian workers usually find sixty per cent of the people they contact end up supporting them.

As you can see from the following example, outlining *specific* steps is crucial. Figure 9.1 is a detailed example of a support plan. You can use the same format in developing your own plan.

Making Specific Requests

The first part of the plan helps you decide which groups to ask. But you also need to decide what specific dollar amount to ask for. For example, you may have a budget of $20,000. Do you simply present that figure in the hope that supporters will know what to

---

Figure 9.1   A support plan

Goals

A. To share my call to ministry with enthusiasm and integrity to potential contributors.

B. To nurture support partners with information from the field and with personal interest in their well-being through regular visits, phone calls and letters.

C. To raise a total of _____ per month in designated support by _____. The following is a list of estimated sources and amounts:

Group	Amount	By (date)
My parents' church	$400/mo.	June 30
My new church	200/mo.	Aug. 15
30 Friends and family at $25/mo.	750/mo.	June 30
Alumni of M.U.	250/mo.	Sept. 1
Local Committee and misc. church contacts	400/mo.	Aug. 15
	$2,000/mo	Sept. 1

1. List the persons to be contacted by mail. If you're just starting, aim for a list of 150-200 names. If you're continuing, add 25-30. Emphasize personal letters rather than printed ones whenever possible.

Person(s)	Letter Type (personal, intro., etc.)	Send (date)
D. Smith P. Jones G. Williams A. Casey	Reception at Jones's for these former classmates; letter of invitation	May 17
B. Eaton R. Gifford L. Kelly P. Pious (. . .)	1. Personal letter 2. Support Request 3. Call to nonresponders Bimonthly prayer letters	May 15 June 15 June 30 Oct./Dec./Feb.
M.U. Alumni (approx. 50)	Alumni letter and news sheet Fund appeal	July 20

2. List below the names, methods (visits, calls, receptions and so on) and timetable for your *personal* contacts with individuals.

Name	Method (note, call, visit)	By (date)

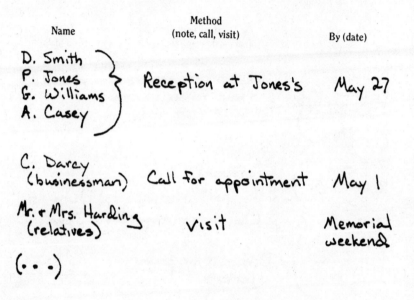

D. Smith
P. Jones
G. Williams
A. Casey   } Reception at Jones's   May 27

C. Darcy
(businessman)   Call for appointment   May 1

Mr. & Mrs. Harding
(relatives)   visit   Memorial
                                      weekend

(. . .)

3. List below special groups (local groups, organizations and so on) to be contacted.

Group	Initial Contact (method)	Contacted By (date)	Follow-up (date)
Midtown Local Committee	call Bill James (chairman)	May 15	May 30
Christian Businessmen's Committee	call Ron Andrews to ask who leads meetings — seek an invitation to speak	June 10	June 15

4. Target at least one to two churches for your extensive personal involvement in a missions conference or other major activity. Aim to raise at least $1,200 to $5,000 annually from these churches. Usually they will be your current and former home churches where you are known well or the church where you will locate in your new community.

List the names of five to ten other churches for long-term contact for support. Remember, it almost always requires two to three personal contacts (*not* letters) and several months to cultivate a church as a donor. Aim for two to five hundred dollars from the churches that seem most interested.

Church Name	Method of Contact	Date
Bethany Church (parents')	1. Call pastor	By May 1
	2. Visit him and missions com.	By May 30
	3. Send request for $4800/yr. (shared at meeting).	By June 5
	4. Share at worship	At June 6 service
Grace Chapel (my new church)	1. Visit pastor,	By May 15
	2. Share with missions com.	By June 15
	3. Display work at Missions conference	Sept. 15
1st Pres. Church 1st Baptist Messiah Church	Call on pastor and ask his advice for further contact	During July 21-28

5. What multimedia, brochures or other resources are needed to implement the preceding plans? By what dates will you need them?

Resource(s)	For Whom	Request (date)
"Unreached Peoples" movie	Bethany and Grace visits	check May 10
General brochures	all contacts	order April 30

6. What training or assistance will you seek from your supervisor, local supporters and/or headquarters personnel?

Ask supervisor to do one day of calls with me as I contact businessmen (referrals).

Ask Bill and Jan Smith to set up reception for current supporters.

Call national office for advice on my prayer card.

7. How will you develop *prayer support* for your support-raising efforts?

Ask 4 Former classmates
to pray weekly For me.

Call by
June 1

8. Translate your timetable entries from the above plans onto a calendar so you can see them in sequence and allot an appropriate amount of time to each task (see sample).

MONTH __May__

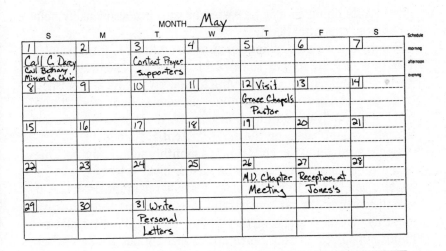

S	M	T	W	T	F	S	Schedule
1 Call C. Darcy, Call Bethany Mission Co. Chair	2	3 Contact Prayer Supporters	4	5	6	7	morning / afternoon / evening
8	9	10	11	12 Visit Grace Chapel's Pastor	13	14	
15	16	17	18	19	20	21	
22	23	24	25	26 M.V. Chapter Meeting	27 Reception at Jones's	28	
29	30	31 Write Personal Letters					

MONTH __June__

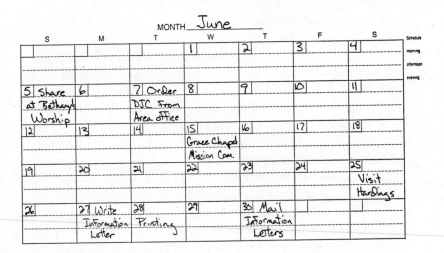

S	M	T	W	T	F	S	Schedule
			1	2	3	4	morning / afternoon / evening
5 Share at Bethany's Worship	6	7 Order DJC from Area office	8	9	10	11	
12	13	14	15 Grace Chapel Mission Com.	16	17	18	
19	20	21	22	23	24	25 Visit Hardings	
26	27 Write Information Letter	28 Printing	29	30 Mail Information Letters			

give? While doing so may be easier for you, it doesn't really help a potential supporter decide.

Shake any fears of asking for firm commitments from people. The apostle Paul sought some of his heaviest commitments, or pledges for help, from people giving to God's work. He admonished them to test their love by giving. His words about sowing and reaping sparingly or bountifully also apply. We should not hesitate to seek similar pledges on the part of potential supporters.

Begin by dividing the budget into a monthly support figure. This is the total amount needed to be raised, divided by twelve. This enables you to talk to people using a smaller amount. People will see they can make an impact and it encourages them to give monthly. We encourage regular giving because it physically reminds supporters of you. Some critics feel annual gifts are wiser since they cut down on the number of transactions between you and donors. But that's precisely our point: regular communication between you and your supporters is what is needed. Regular support facilitates this.

Once the monthly budget amount is set, how will you know what dollar amount to ask for? Our approach emphasizes what each person can give, rather than what you need. By this we mean to take the donor's interest, occupation and other giving into account before requesting an amount. Such boldness may seem manipulative, but it's not. People want guidance in deciding what to give. But *they* are still the ones who make the final decision.

Students are an excellent example of how workers often shy away from a specific request. Some avoid asking students because they believe students have no money. Others, realizing many students work and have extra money, ask for a ten-dollar-per-month gift. Many students can meet this specific request. Likewise, those friends and family most empathetic and able to give can be asked for fifty to sixty dollars or more. Your home church, for example, can be asked for at least one to two hundred dollars per month. Again, you're not coercing people to give, you are simply suggesting an amount they might handle.

Years ago, a friend began raising support by asking others to give "regularly." Many who were inexperienced with giving outside their church had no idea what he meant. Weekly? Biweekly? Annually? Similarly, some of his friends and family had no idea what amount to give. His church began by giving one hundred dollars per month. He found out that, had he asked, they were prepared to give more. Similar experiences will teach you to be specific in your requests for support. Consider each friend, church and relative's potential for support, and ask for the maximum amount the Lord might lead each to give.

You should seek a commitment from each supporter as to their intended giving frequency and amount. We refer to the commitment to give as a *faith promise*. The card in Figure 9.2 is what Inter-Varsity staff use to collect support. The card is given (usually with a business reply envelope) to a potential supporter when he or she is asked to give. After filling it out, the donor returns the bottom portion of the card, along with their first gift, to the national office. It is then forwarded to the staff member for record keeping. The new donor keeps the top portion of the card as a reminder of his or her commitment. Sometimes people will give without your having a record of their intent. In those cases it's still best to seek their commitment—either send a partner card or call them. Having a record of each person's commitment will help you match donor support with your need.

Once you have a person's commitment in hand, keep track of it. Compare your monthly gift print-out with each person's commitment. If a person misses two gifts in a row, send him or her a gentle reminder. This practice fulfills the purpose behind obtaining gift commitments. It not only shows supporters you keep accurate records, it also reflects your desire to help them support you.

What about prayer commitments? If you're genuinely concerned that people pray regularly for you and your ministry, why not seek pledges for prayer? You may want to seek prayer partners at a different time than when you do financial support raising. You don't want potential supporters to think they have a prayer-or-

Dear Friend,

Inter-Varsity Christian Fellowship is the oldest and largest interdenominational campus ministry—committed to reaching a world of
students for Jesus Christ.

Our campus staff seek to establish, assist and encourage groups of
Christian students on over 900 campuses and universities across the
United States.

We are supported primarily by the financial gifts and prayers of men
and women interested in our ministry. Please prayerfully consider
becoming a member of our support team.

Inter-Varsity Christian Fellowship   233 Langdon   Madison, Wisconsin
(608) 257-0263

☐ I will pray regularly for you.
☐ I will begin supporting you for $ _____
each ☐ month ☐ quarter ☐ year, until _____, 19 _____.
☐ I will **continue** supporting you for $ _____
each ☐ month ☐ quarter ☐ year, until _____, 19 _____.
☐ I can't support you now, but keep me informed about your ministry.
☐ Please remove my name from your mailing list.

Name_____ Phone (_____)_____

Address _____

City _____ State _____ Zip _____

Make checks payable to Inter-Varsity Christian Fellowship, clearly indicate your
gift for the work of **John Smith.** All contributions are tax-deductible and will be
receipted.

I understand that for my gifts to be tax-deductible they will be used solely for the
salaries and expenses of the named staff worker or project under the direction
and control of the Board of Trustees of Inter-Varsity Christian Fellowship of the USA.

Inter-Varsity Christian Fellowship   233 Langdon   Madison, Wisconsin 53703
(608) 257-0263

*Figure 9.2   Inter-Varsity's support card is one example of a "pledge" card for obtaining a
commitment from supporters.*

money choice. Set a realistic goal for the number of people you want praying, and how often. One overseas mission agency requires all its missionaries to have twenty committed prayer partners. Ask individuals to commit themselves to pray for a different aspect of your ministry once a week. A word of caution—vary the requests in some kind of prayer calendar or special tear-off section of your monthly reports. Then keep track of answers to prayer and report them to your supporters.

Schedule and Evaluation

The first page of the support plan asked for the date when the support goal would be met. Now we need to take a similar step for each component of the plan.

In the sample plan, a home church and a new church were targeted to be contacted. In order to acquire a support promise (or at least a hearing) by the target date of September 1, we would need to plan to make initial contacts months in advance. The same is true for family, friends, alumni and other groups.

Look at a calendar to see when to begin each step. In order to give people an outside time limit of two months to decide whether or not they will support you, and let's say with a target of September 1, they need to be asked by July 1. If you plan to send a letter of introduction before asking each group for support, you should mail it by June 1. To mail by June 1, the letter needs to be written by mid-May and printed by the end of the month. Write out specific due dates for each of these steps.

Appointments or a letter requesting support comes next. Call those you plan to visit within a week after they've received their introductory letter (June 7). Set up appointments for the rest of the month (group them by areas of your city to save time). You can write, print and mail your support-raising letter either in conjunction with the May introductory letter or shortly thereafter. Simply work the steps backward from your target date. By doing this you'll get a better idea of how much time support raising will take. Make changes if the dates don't seem realistic.

Once you've confirmed due dates for each step, write them into your daily calendar. Planning has little value if it isn't specific, realistic and adhered to. Ask your supervisor or a coworker to help you stick to the dates and steps in your plan. Make sure they're informed so they can help and hold you accountable.

Evaluation and a Plan B are the final components to a plan. You are expected to have one hundred per cent of your support raised by a particular date (before boarding your plane overseas). What will you do if it's the month before you leave and you're only at fifty per cent? If you plan ahead you shouldn't have to worry. Too many Christian workers make a few appointments and then wait— and wait—and wait. Support raising is a *continuous* process. You need to follow up on every contact made. Call those you've written or visited and get firm replies. Then, two months before your deadline, take a reading of your progress. If some people haven't yet replied, call them. If others have said they would give but haven't sent their first gift, call or write and remind them.

Plan B is a series of alternative steps to take should all initial contacts be exhausted. The first step in Plan B comes as you talk to friends, family and churches. Ask them for *referrals,* names of others who may be interested in supporting you that you don't know about. This expands your contact base. It's sometimes awkward to ask for referrals. Most of the time we forget to ask— especially if the person we're asking has just turned us down for support. Everyone is usually open to help in another way. "Do you know of any other people—friends, perhaps—who might be interested in my ministry?" If it's at all possible, ask the person if he or she would introduce you to the person they refer. This is especially helpful in an unfamiliar church. Your credibility can be enhanced with an introduction from the pastor or person you know in the congregation. Add referrals to your plan and contact them as you go along.

A second part of Plan B requires the help of your supervisor. Supervisors frequently have access to lists of churches and individuals who used to be interested in your agency's work or who might give to different parts of it. Try to determine their interests (either from your supervisor or support records) before making contact. Introduce yourself and your mission. For people who have stopped giving, ask if they would renew their giving. They may have stopped simply because the organization stopped communicating with them. For those who give to another part of the ministry, thank them for their support and ask if they'd consider a special gift for your work.

Next Steps
Fill out your own plan based on the example on pages 82-89. Be specific, realistic and stick to the steps and dates you set.

10

Donor Nurture

Many of us take the words *thank you* for granted. If someone gives us a gift, we thank them—the same with a compliment. We thank the person who holds a door for us. We thank our children, a friend, the postman and the paperboy. Eventually "thanks" ends up meaning less than we intended.

We run into a similar predicament with supporters. Here we have a special group of people who care enough about us and our ministry to pray and give regular support. We admit they're a great bunch of people—worthy of our appreciation. Yet amid speaking engagements, travel and details of ministry we end up sending feeble words of thanks. Regardless of how we feel about them, we end up showing little gratitude.

There's a yearning to do something more—perhaps write personally more often—but how personal can you be with one hundred supporters?

Supporter Care
The answer to this predicament is to demonstrate care for supporters in some of the same ways you've felt needed and appreciated in the past. In short, *nurture* your supporters. Give tangible signs of your concern for them.

Begin by taking your supporters' needs into account. Many

times we get so wrapped up in our ministry we can no longer relate well to those we care for most. Our needs, rather than our supporters' needs, become paramount. Most of your supporters will probably have little orientation to your ministry. They're not as immersed in the day-to-day activities and professional language as you are. You need to stop and reorient your thinking about the ministry before contacting supporters. Don't change what you intend to say to them, simply explain things in terms they can understand and appreciate. In a way, describe the ministry as though you were an outsider. This practice comes easily when you strive for two-way communication. Show concern for your supporters as people who have more interests than just your ministry. Seek out their interests. Ask questions. Listen.

Give your supporters options for involvement in your ministry. Prayer and money are not the only two elements of support. As you discover their interests and talents, make use of them. Invite a donor who's interested in Bible exposition to help you write a talk. Tell your accountant friend that you would appreciate her help in budgeting for a conference. Seek advice, counsel, physical assistance, teaching and encouragement. Some may not be interested or have the time (this may be the case for you as well). That's fine. They will at least appreciate being asked.

Keep in regular contact. Supporters don't like to be ignored. Schedule time to write, call or visit, if possible (or have someone else do it on your behalf), every couple of months. Make the effort to thank a person as often and as soon as he or she gives to your work. Evidence shows that the sooner a gift is acknowledged, the sooner a person is likely to give again. Remember, you are in no small way competing for the attention of even your most faithful supporters. Make your presence felt through regular contact.

Second, try showing thanks. Sometimes gifts—such as a book or a cassette tape of a talk—are effective thank-yous. Stand out from the crowd of people who say "thank you" so often. Let your supporters feel appreciated by the way you treat them and the things you do for them.

Another idea is to send a stamped, self-addressed postcard asking for their prayer requests. Pray through these requests in a month's devotions. Such acts of kindness will make the difference between simple expressions and heartfelt thanks.

Other suggestions take this idea a step further and depend on how open a person you are. Pull supporters into the ministry by sharing "inside information" with them. By this we mean letting them know the real joys and frustrations of working with other believers in ministry. Share strategies for campus expansion and ask for suggestions. Give them the big picture of where the organization is headed. Several months ago when we were in the midst of planning a new alumni program, a coworker asked some of his postgraduate supporters for suggestions. They were flattered to think they would have a part in the plan.

Prayer Letters

Any time missionaries talk about thanking supporters, the term *prayer letter* comes up. It's become our all-purpose means of communication. But its function to inform never changes. We've read hundreds of prayer letters over the past several years—few of which were exciting. Most of us who write to supporters have a lot to get off our chests. We travel and toil through months without writing. Then, when we can no longer stand the pressure of news and burdens (and prayer letter deadlines), words suddenly burst onto pages destined for our supporters. But little of what we write is really news for prayer. And little is personal. Brian used to tell his supporters where he had been for the past three months, and how he had gotten there. One day he read one of his own prayer letters and realized it was just a boring itinerary. Others we've read are bleak with the writer's depression and despair. People reading such a letter are certain to go away with the world's burdens on their shoulders. That should not be the intention of writing.

Prayer letters aren't for therapy. We describe letters more functionally—to share news and feelings about the ministry *for the reader's benefit*. Keep that last point in mind as you sit down to write. View the ministry from their perspective. And don't write with more than one purpose in mind. Here we're talking about informing and encouraging supporters, not asking for money. Save that subject for a special communique. (To better understand the distinctions between prayer and fundraising letters see chapter seven.)

The content of a prayer letter can vary widely. Keep in mind, though, that news should be recent. Don't draw attention to your tardiness in writing. Letters which begin, "Sorry I haven't written for *so* long . . . ," let readers know they're in for an earful of news and blues. Supporters also have busy schedules. Instead, speak in terms of today, yesterday and tomorrow. Notice how newspaper writers make their articles sound like everything either just happened or is pending. Follow their lead.

As we said earlier about letters for fundraising, use a personal style. Speak in terms of you (singular) and me. Letters that address a group read like they're directed toward no one in particular. Your supporters already know they're not alone. Being impersonal is difficult when writing to a friend.

Choose subjects carefully. Are your supporters interested in your ministry, your family or both? If your family is part of your ministry you've already answered the question. Just make the connection evident.

When speaking of ministry, share plans, progress and failures. No one makes great strides every week. Write honestly, using feelings as well as thoughts.

As we suggested in chapter seven, use stories about real people. People like to read about people. Rather than write "the conference was a blessing," share a story about one participant. Let the reader draw his or her own conclusions.

Say you decided to write about a new believer's experiences at a conference you helped lead. Will you interview her or simply narrate her activities? Another possibility is for her to write the letter for you. Regardless of the method chosen, be sure to talk about the *feelings* involved in her experience. Stay away from the day-in-the-life-of-Sally approach.

Similarly, try to make the story compelling to the average reader. For example, relate a story of salvation in the life of one of the people you're working with to the reader's salvation experience. "Think for a moment of the joy you had on first reading and understanding the Bible. One of my students, Jeffrey, just told me what it meant to him last night . . . ," is one example.

A few final thoughts on format and style. Don't be cute when packaging a message. Stay away from red or green paper at Christmas time. Don't write in calligraphy. Instead, be creative in other ways. Occasionally abandon ministry letterhead in favor of personal stationery—preferably something with a distinct message and design. The same holds true for size, colors and print. Everyone receives letters typed on eight-and-a-half-by-eleven-inch white paper. Dare to be different. Try writing postcards, or write on smaller sheets of paper. All gifts can be acknowledged with a postcard (most cities have hundreds to choose from). Many use motel stationery for sending news when attending a conference or meeting in another city. It gives the recipient a sense of immediacy and presence.

The Communications Calendar

The Communications Calendar (figure 10.1) is a tool for planning what and when to communicate with supporters. Inter-Varsity staff are required to write supporters at least every other month. Planning topics and making dates a year in advance are definitely worth the effort. Supporters can often read the haste written into an eleventh-hour prayer letter. Also, carving out time on a calendar in advance is more easily handled than last-minute scheduling. And when you know ahead what the topic of your next month's letter will be, it is easy to gather the pertinent information as you go along—easier than scraping it up ten minutes before writing.

Look at your calendar of events before rounding out your letter schedule. Are there special conferences, ministry concerns or a furlough coming up? Pencil them into the writing schedule. Gath-

Communications Calendar

YEAR: _____

Month	Other forms of communication to your team*	Mailing Goal	Date Mailed	Proposed Theme	Ideas/Artwork/Pictures/Comments/Etc.
July					
August					
September					
October					
November					
December					
January					
February					
March					
April					
May					
June					

*Other forms of communication: personal contact, telephone calls, postcards to a majority of the team, Christmas cards, gifts. INFORM THEM, EXPRESS LOVE AND APPRECIATION, MINISTER TO THEM

Figure 10.1   Plan how and when you'll get in touch with supporters with the help of a Communications Calendar. Plan some sort of contact (personal note, call, etc.) at least once a month, if possible.

er information for your letter while in the midst of the work you'll describe. For example, say you were planning to write about a new Christian who attended a conference you led. Take time during the conference to talk to him. Ask him to describe how he's feeling—how the conference is helping him grow. Take notes. By the time you arrive home, your letter will almost be complete.

Plan topics to coincide with seasonal activities, and put them into your calendar. The same applies for any gift books you plan to send supporters. Write in the month you'll send them so you can order ahead of time.

Show your gratitude by nurturing supporters with all the attention you can afford. Make each person's contribution an experience to remember. Don't be afraid to expand opportunities for their involvement. View your work from their perspective. Make them feel thanked. Listen as well as share. This personal, donor-centered appreciation will go a long way toward building relationships and expanding your support.

Paul is our example: "I have received full payment and even more; I am amply supplied, now that I have received from Epaphroditus the gifts you sent. They are a fragrant offering, an acceptable sacrifice, pleasing to God. And my God will meet all your needs according to his glorious riches in Christ Jesus" (Phil 4:18-19 NIV).

Next Steps
1. Once you've begun to receive support, plan your own Communications Calendar for the coming year.

2. Exchange prayer letters and other ideas on donor nurture with fellow workers. Adapt them to your cause.

11

Special Topics

This chapter will cover less common situations and means of support raising. Special circumstances, whether asking for support in an urban, minority church or from a wealthy donor, dictate special procedures. We will outline the basic steps in handling support raising in these contexts.

Students and Alumni

For some organizations working with college or high-school students, alumni and students are a key source for support. Many graduates who were helped by Young Life, Navigators or other organizations may look back with fond memories, but that's all. There's little reason for them to stay in touch, especially if we aren't keeping in touch with them. Yet as we seek more funds for an ever-expanding budget, students and alumni can be a great help.

An organized approach to alumni work begins by dividing the task between current seniors and graduates. Compile lists in both categories, using student and graduate records to jog your memory. The key to a good alumni program is a well-conceived and maintained filing system. Some use file cards to keep track of graduates. But this is one excellent application for a personal computer as well. Even the smallest colleges and youth organiza·

tions are now keeping alumni records on computer. We recommend that you either keep your files on a friend's computer or, if your budget will allow, buy your own. Talk to someone in your agency's data-processing department or a local vendor for a recommended make and model.

File each person's name, home address, year of graduation, school attended, major, staff worker and notes on their involvement with your organization. These alumni characteristics are commonly called attributes. The person's name, school and year of graduation are the attributes most often referred to in a file. Be sure to collect and record them in an accessible part of the files.

As your memory for names fades, contact a few of the student leaders for each of the last several years at each school. Ask for names and addresses of former friends from their campus group. Then compare lists.

Finding names is easy. Attaching current addresses is another story. Try several routes to complete your lists: First, check with your organization's gifts-processing department. Some people may be listed on their computer as donors or prayer partners. Second, ask the alumni you know for help. Their network of friends will extend far and wide. Even if you obtain only a name and a date of graduation, cross reference it with a school's current address records. Even a parent's address is worth a try. Third, contact former staff who served at your school. Fourth, check with the alumni office at your school. Even if the graduates never joined their alumni association, their office should have current addresses. However, usually only the smallest colleges maintain records of student involvement in religious groups.

Once you have basic information on seniors and graduates, offer them something tangible. With the first group, call attention to the present. With the other, remind them of their past to bring them into the present. We suggest two activities.

First, plan a banquet or dessert for seniors at your school. In May, alumni volunteers have held a seniors' appreciation dinner for the University of Wisconsin Inter-Varsity chapter. The dinner and program have three purposes: first, to make the seniors feel needed and appreciated for leadership in their chapter; second, to prepare them for what is to come after school; and third, to ask them to support the ministry from which they've benefited. Articles on work ethics, marriage, family and church involvement are handed out. Alumni from the working world have an opportunity to share things they know which will help seniors in transition. The alumni's perspectives and credibility are priceless.

As the campus missionary, spend a few moments explaining the scope of your agency's work and your role in it. Remind students of their growth and of the growth that will take place in students after they leave.

At the close of the program, give them practical options for helping you. Ask them to keep in touch, pledge to your support and to refer people or resources helpful to you in your ministry.

Our second suggestion is a tool for contact with both groups— an alumni newsletter. If a quarterly newsletter isn't the kind of thing you have time to do, look for an enthusiastic alumnus to help out. Its purpose is to give alumni something in return for their support. You can use it as a resource for club news, books you recommend, camps they can attend and student trends.

Use the newsletter as a means of keeping addresses current. Once you've lost track of alumni, relocating them is hard. And since some cannot contribute right away, keep nondonors on the list for a few years. Mailing to extra names is worth the investment.

Use the newsletter to make requests for prayer and financial support as well. Make the requests specific, and provide a means for response (reply envelope).

When the first newsletter is finished, include in it a special mailing. Send a copy of the newsletter, your organization's donor magazine and a personal letter inviting them into the alumni fellowship. Though it may have been a while since they've had a chance to recall their school days, remind them of the growth that took place in their lives. People don't forget those who had an impact on their spiritual walk. Use this reference as a springboard to request involvement in your ministry. Explain the benefits of keeping in touch and contributing to the work.

A few final points can make your alumni experience more satisfying. When you hear of alumni in another part of the country, take a minute to let the local staff person know who and where they are. If you're open about giving alumni referrals to other staff members, they will return the favor. Neither of you will lose by keeping alumni informed of all opportunities to help.

Teach the students about tithing *now*. Don't simply give them a handout at graduation. Every student should know what Scripture says about "contributing to the needs of the saints" and practice doing so before they graduate.

Finally, don't worry about the alumni names you can't get. For whatever reason, some people simply cannot be tracked down. Any organized attempt to keep alumni involved will be well worth the effort.

Urban and Minority Support Raising

In practice, support raising varies from a Japanese American community to a Black community, from a Baptist church to an Episcopal church, and in many other settings. Here, we will limit our comments to urban and minority support raising. In this context we have found that traditional methods work only marginally well. Resources, experiences and language are different. Consequently, the urban or minority Christian worker must approach the task differently.

Two basic approaches in such support raising are a minority missionary attempting to raise support from his or her own minority church community, or a nonminority missionary attempting to raise support from the ethnic church and community in which he or she ministers. Both call for the missionary to realize certain characteristics of the urban or minority church community as they are approached for support.

The local churches are typically the focal point for missions concern, information and giving among minorities. In this regard things haven't changed much from the eighteenth and nineteenth centuries when European immigrants flooded American shores. Their national identity was retained with the help of the community, or ethnic, church. Today, Hispanic and Asian immigrants—and even some established several-generation American citizens—find their church to be a place to learn from and adapt to the majority American culture, as well as a place to retain their cultural identity.

If you are a nonminority worker, be cautious when approaching the minority church. Work to communicate so that you aren't misunderstood in your purposes for mission and in what you are asking of the church. When you make a mistake, apologize, change and keep coming. People often won't reject you if they know that you have good intentions and are open to learn. The endorsement of an opinion leader in the church community—usually the pastor or a key layperson—is important if you are to be welcomed and heard. Let them see and experience your track record. Tell them of your ambitions for mission work within the minority community. Then let them speak on your behalf and introduce you to others in the church and community.

Do your homework before you approach the church. Check their denomination's history and ministry in the community, as well as their traditional pattern for giving. Don't assume they give a certain way just because you're from the same denomination or tradition. Request support from the church in a way they are used to giving to others. In other words, if special offerings are their practice, don't insist on monthly (budgeted) support. Get the pastor excited, let him get the congregation excited, and then ask for a specific gift that fits their pattern of giving and your need.

One of the chief reasons Christian workers rarely ask for support from minority churches and communities is because they presume the churches are poor. Not all minority churches are poor. We shrink from asking for support from those with whom we're working simply because we don't feel they can give enough. But that isn't a sufficient reason. Even in extreme poverty and famine, the Macedonian church gave both to the Lord's work in other churches and to Paul's needs as a missionary. There is also the account of the poor widow who gave all her money to the Lord's work. Realizing that a minority church may be poor will help in your approach and in the amount you request of the congregation. Be humble, but don't hesitate to inform them of your work and ask for support.

For some minority churches in the United States, the idea of sending a missionary—or supporting a domestic one—is new. Be sensitive to this in the way you introduce yourself as a missionary and in how you describe your organization's view of sending missionaries in domestic situations.

They also may not understand how you, if you're a nonminority person or are perceived to work for a "white" organization, would have much of a ministry in a minority setting. Unless you explain fully, they might have a hard time grasping what you want to do. Cite the need for your particular witness—wherever it may be. For example, if you'll be working with primarily Hispanic inner-city kids, ask a few Hispanic churches to support you. You may explain that the children need a Christian witness and example to strengthen their view of the church and community. Family and community are of particular importance to most Hispanic churches.

Christian workers must pay attention to the priorities and distinctives of the minority church and community. For example, one of the key issues for missions support in the Black church is *social justice*. It is an issue because of past and present conditions in the Black community. Evangelism (carrying the message to the people) is not considered separate from social concerns (meeting physical needs and fighting injustice). The missionary representing an organization with a historical lack of emphasis on social concerns must choose his or her words carefully. Without a proper endorsement from within the church or adequate explanation from outside, you may be misunderstood. A poor presentation of total mission will not only result in rejection of support, it will enhance subtle differences in ministry. One is disappointing; the other is devastating.

Each church has its own agenda. Some may only support a missionary coming from within their church or with the same cultural background. It may have nothing to do with you, your mission or your organization. They simply follow a policy (self-consciously or not) that happens to only support one group. The best policy is to "test the waters" with a friend who attends the church before you approach them. And if you don't get a reception at this time, move on to the next one.

Approach a minority church or community *humbly* for support. You and your supporting organization may have to broaden your purposes—or at least the language used—and improve your track record in minority ministry. One must be sensitive and patient to get a hearing for support.

Large Gifts

Donors who send large gifts are special people—not better than other donors, just special people in need of special care-and-feeding.

We mentioned the eighty-twenty rule for raising money from churches in chapter eight. This also applies to people who give large donations. More time, skill and effort are usually involved in attracting a large gift than in attracting a small one. Conversely, the large donor can sometimes give as much as one hundred per cent of your support in one gift.

Let's discuss some guidelines for attracting such a donor. First, you must be willing and able to invest time in seeking the gift. People don't give huge gifts on a whim. You need to cultivate a relationship with the person. Patience is essential.

Second, you must go where the large donors are. Unless you already know a wealthy potential donor, chances are you won't meet one walking down the street. Seek out people in your church, community or local business organizations.

Third, you must be very sensitive to the large donor's interests and concerns. Often in our attempts to *not* treat the large donor in a favorable way, we end up offending them. Wealthy people may be like you deep down, but on the surface they usually have pressure, responsibility and time constraints that are hard to imagine. Express genuine interest by seeking out their interests and backgrounds. Wealthy people are, in many cases, interested in the present and future leadership of the country. If you minister to those future leaders, all you need to do is match the concern of the donors who give large amounts with your present ministry. Empathy is the key.

Fourth, be alert to suggest a plan for giving that can best be adapted to the prospective donor's situation. Large cash gifts of over a thousand dollars are rare. Deferred gifts, such as stocks and bonds or trusts, are more prevalent among large donors (see Planned Giving below). And both come more frequently at the end of a calendar or fiscal year when taxes are a concern.

Pray for your prospect. Your goal is to get the person involved in your ministry. If there are obstacles in getting to know or minister to him or her, pray for them to be removed. Finally, pray for yourself—that you would be alert, caring, patient and persistent as you foster a support relationship.

A request for a large financial gift is always made face to face. Prepare yourself to meet the person in his or her office or home. You must be prepared to state your case in as little as ten minutes—even if you've scheduled a thirty-minute appointment. The person may be very busy, so be flexible and concise.

Once you have obtained a substantial gift, thank the donor. Again, don't let your attitude suggest favoritism. Be careful not to alienate your other supporters. Show thanks in a way the supporter will appreciate. An immediate personal visit is not too much to expect. If you are genuinely thankful you will go out of your way to care for the person and show appreciation for him or her *and* the gift. Remember, the person is most important.

Planned Giving
What would you do if someone wanted to write your ministry into their will? Or if a friend gave you thirty shares of IBM stock? Cash

isn't the only type of gift. Each year millions of dollars of stock are given for religious causes. Some donors give part of an estate, a gift loan, jewelry—even cemetery plots! While such donations may seem odd, many missionaries have benefited from their cash value. It's important not only to know how to handle these gifts, but also how one can go about acquiring them.

This is usually done with the help of a planned giving or development department within your organization. Through planned giving, people can take advantage of legal methods to fulfill their charitable intentions to give and reduce the tax burden on their heirs. Legal arrangements can also be made to handle transfers of possessions like a car, a house or jewelry. Donors benefit through a tax deduction, while a staff member benefits by receiving a large gift.

Several avenues for planned giving now exist for supporters. Check with your planned-giving department for details on how to process these gifts. The following is a list of the most common methods of planned giving.

Current Giving. These include gifts of stock, property, life insurance and other material goods. If the gift is something you or your organization can use, keep it. The donor will be receipted after you inform the office of the donor's name and address, and the date and description of gift. If the gift is unusable, such as jewelry, coins or stamps, it can be sold, and the cash transferred to the missionary's account. All nonprofit organizations follow similar procedures. The process for handling gifts of stock are more complex. Since the steps involved may vary from organization to organization, we suggest contacting your planned giving office before accepting a stock gift.

Annuities. Annuity plans are for people who want to give money to your work, while still providing income for themselves or a survivor (should the donor die). The annuity usually gives a person increased income, while allowing them considerable tax advantages that will save them money. The donor gives a lump sum to your organization. Your organization then agrees to pay the donor a certain amount on a yearly basis. The organization then invests the money, combining it with other funds, to yield a higher interest, and thus, income for ministry. There are two types of annuities. The regular gift annuity is most beneficial for people forty-five years old or older. The deferred gift annuity benefits those younger because it defers income until a later date, usually at retirement, when taxable income is reduced.

Trusts. As the name implies, this is a property interest held or entrusted by one person for the benefit of another. A donor may set aside a large amount of money (like an inheritance) into a trust. Depending on the type of trust established, interest that would normally go to taxes could instead be designated for your organization. Trusts can be revocable (temporary), irrevocable (permanent) or living (current).

Estate Planning. This includes any planned method for setting aside property or money for your immediate or eventual benefit. Wills, trusts and life insurance are just three examples of estate plans. Most of your supporters probably already have a will, the most basic form of estate planning. Encourage your more devoted supporters to consider writing your ministry into their will.

Loans. Anyone can place money on deposit to your organization to provide low-cost funds for your work. Under such an agreement, regular income is paid to the donor at an agreed rate of interest (usually below the current rates). You may withdraw the money at any time for any reason. If loan money isn't withdrawn before the donor's death, it becomes a gift to your organization. A loan arrangement with some of your supporters may help you overcome a deficit or expand a team's ministry.

People are supporting you for a variety of reasons. Most give money; some consider the tax benefits in doing so. Yet everyone could undoubtedly give more if they considered alternative ways of giving. Even if their monthly support funds are already allocated, chances are your supporters could give more through planned giving. Let them know the options. But first check what your organization offers through planned giving.

Foundations

Many think of foundations as the financial saviors of Christian work. With less federal money available to secular nonprofit institutions, more organizations have found themselves competing for private dollars. Foundations have been their main target.

A foundation is a nonprofit, tax-exempt organization whose basic purpose is to promote certain causes by distributing financial gifts. The foundation holds in trust certain assets, such as common stocks, bonds, land or improved property. The broad purpose is to conserve these assets, and in some instances add to them. Each has a governing board of directors who see to it that income from the assets is properly distributed to achieve the aims and desires of the owner of the foundation. The purposes are usually outlined in the bylaws and stated purpose of the foundation's charter.

There are approximately 30,000 foundations in the United States. The 200 largest have assets totaling more than the combined assets of the other 29,800. The largest twenty comprise the greatest majority of foundation assets in America. Over 4,000 foundations have either stated or proved an interest in donating to religious nonprofit organizations.

Foundations vary by size as well as function. Some, such as the Ford and Rockefeller foundations, have professional staff. Smaller private foundations rely on family members to manage their more limited assets. There are four distinct types of foundations. First is the large, general purpose foundation. While they have specific objectives, they often support a wide variety of causes.

Corporate foundations, such as Monsanto and McDonnell Douglas, often limit their giving to promoting good relations with employees and customers. Community foundations are a collective of small trusts banded together to support a local community. And then there are the thousands of family foundations. Their purposes (or charters) include religion, education, art and medicine. Most are funded by part of a family fortune set aside to promote the concern of the family or one of its members.

The majority of large foundations are found in New York City

(6,000). But, with few exceptions, there are several hundred in every state. (Missouri, for example, has over four hundred foundations, each with assets of less than one million dollars.) Most are clustered around cities in proximity to large banks, trust companies, law offices and industrial corporations.

Family foundations are more inclined to support Christian work. This may be true because the donor is a Christian or because its charter is unrestricted. They are also generally more approachable, less well known and less subject to public pressure. Many may simply share a concern for Philadelphians, single parents, college students or Peruvians.

Evangelical causes rarely receive big foundation grants. And even the small grant is not easy to obtain. Much research, development and painstaking work is often required to just get an initial hearing. Small courtesy grants may or may not come quickly. Larger grants can take up to two or three years to obtain.

Nevertheless, a great opportunity exists to obtain foundation grants. With about four thousand family foundations interested in religious causes, your agency has probably only begun to tap resources for giving.

Before you try to obtain a foundation grant of your own, it's essential that you or the project in question be on your organization's budget. Then answer the following questions:

1. Is there a valid need for the grant? Can you clearly state it? Will the project or staff appointment be accomplished if the grant is obtained?

2. Does the project fall clearly within your agency's purposes?

3. Does it (or do you) carry a supervisor's endorsement?

4. What are the details surrounding the project? How will it meet the given need?

5. What is your complete budget for the project? (If it carries over a period of years, give a brief budget for each year.)

6. When is your budget deadline?

7. Do you have any supplementary information, such as letters, clippings, photographs or history? (Include them.)

Do *not* attempt to contact any foundation on your own. Once you've compiled information on your project, contact your organization's foundation office. They are best equipped to prepare the proposal and make contacts with appropriate foundations— either with you or on your behalf. The process of proposing a grant is often lengthy and certainly delicate. Contact their office for more information.

Epilog

There is eternal value in the basic ministry to which we are called. People will come to Christ and grow in him. But do we also see the eternal value in enabling others to take part in our work? People will stand with us in prayer, emotionally and with gifts. It is satisfying for friends to know that, through us, they support a work of God in this world.

The benefits to our supporters are also eternal. Scripture states that those who "give but cannot go" have great value in God's sight. They will be blessed for their obedience and participation (Phil 4:18-19). Though Scripture does say God provides for those who give, this is not meant to obligate them. The difference is in one's intention. If we ask others to support our work because they will get blessed financially in return, heaven help us. People should give out of a desire to see others helped—to see *their* increase. That's the primary motivation. God will bless them (and us) tangibly and spiritually in return. We cannot demand it.

God has established a beautiful pattern for communication and involvement between himself and us. The interrelationship between us and our supporters is one way this is demonstrated. We begin our support raising by first asking God for provision. Rarely does God answer our prayers without enlisting the help of others. Most of the time God inspires and equips others to be the answer to our prayers. We ask God, and others. He provides others with the means and desire to help us. And we complete the cycle by thanking God and our supporters, and keeping them informed of our work. We advise asking for and seeking support—even though some have raised support without asking. They are the exception and not the rule. The point is to not deny the value of interdependence and support among believers. Prayer and financial gifts are two ways people can be involved in our ministry. Simply give them the opportunity to help.

God calls us into our mission and support ministry *together*. Accept your calling with this balance in mind.

Suggested Reading

The following books, periodicals and papers are highly recommended for further reading. They are listed by categories pertinent to missionary support raising.

History

Grubb, Norman. *C. T. Studd.* Grand Rapids, Mich.: Zondervan, 1941.

Kane, J. Herbert. *Life and Work on the Mission Field.* Grand Rapids, Mich.: Baker, 1980.

Latourette, Kenneth. *A History of Christianity.* Vol. 1. New York: Harper & Row, 1975.

————. *A History of the Expansion of Christianity.* Vols. 1-2, 7. Grand Rapids, Mich.: Zondervan, 1971.

Powell, Luther. *Money and the Church.* New York: Association Press, 1962.

Steer, Roger. *George Müller: Delighted in God!* Carol Stream, Ill.: Harold Shaw, 1981.

Taylor, Mr. & Mrs. Howard. *The Story of the China Inland Mission.* Vol. 1. London: Marshall Morgan and Scott, 1983.

Taylor, Mrs. Howard. *William Borden.* Chicago: Moody, 1980.

Stewardship

Ellul, Jacques. *Money & Power.* Translated by LaVonne Neff. Downers Grove, Ill.: InterVarsity Press, 1984.

McClanen, Don. *Stewardship Challenges for Ministering to Affluent Persons.* Ministry of Money, Inc. (MOMI), 11301 Neelsville Church Rd., Germantown, MD 20874.

O'Connor, Elizabeth. *Letters to Scattered Pilgrims.* New York: Harper & Row, 1979; especially chapter two, "On Money" and chapter three, "More on Money."

Snow, Catherine. *Writing a Money Autobiography.* MOMI, 11301 Neelsville Church Rd., Germantown, MD 20874.

Vinkemulder, Yvonne. *Enrich Your Life.* Downers Grove, Ill.: InterVarsity Press,

1972.

Webley, Simon. *How to Give Away Your Money.* Downers Grove, Ill.: InterVarsity Press, 1978.

Weborg, John. *God & Mammon.* MOMI, 11301 Neelsville Church Rd., Germantown, MD 20874.

Support Audiences/Case Statement

Engel, James. *How Can I Get Them to Listen?* Grand Rapids, Mich.: Zondervan, 1977.

Ries, Al, and Trout, Jack. *Positioning: The Battle for Your Mind.* New York: McGraw-Hill, 1980.

Writing Letters/Communication Tools

Mack, Karin, and Skjei, Eric. *Overcoming Writing Blocks.* Los Angeles: J. P. Tarcher, 1979.

Pocket Pal. International Paper Co., P.O. Box 100, Church Street Station, New York, NY 10046.

Strunk, William, Jr., and White, E. B. *The Elements of Style.* New York: Macmillan, 1979.

Winkler, G.P., ed. *The Associated Press Stylebook.* Write to AP Newsfeatures, 50 Rockefeller Plaza, New York, NY 10020.

Zinsser, William. *On Writing Well.* 2d ed. New York: Harper & Row, 1980.

General

Hales, Edward, and Youngren, Alan. *Your Money, Their Ministry: A Guide to Responsible Christian Giving.* Grand Rapids, Mich.: Eerdmans, 1981.

Kurzig, Carol. *Foundation Fundamentals: A Guide for Grantseekers.* New York: Foundation Center, 1981.

Perri and Ardman. *Woman's Day Book of Fund Raising.* New York: St. Martin's Press, 1980.

Peters, Thomas J., and Waterman, Robert H., Jr. *In Search of Excellence.* "Close to the Customer," chapter 6. New York: Harper & Row, 1982.

Piguet, Leo. *Fund Raising.* National Institute for Campus Ministries, 1979.

Sharpe, Robert F. *Before You Give Another Dime. . . .* Nashville: Nelson, 1979.

Periodicals

Communicator's Journal—A bimonthly magazine of applied communications. Frequently contains articles helpful to anyone in the communications field. P.O. Box 602, Downtown Station, Omaha, NE 68101.

Currents—The monthly publication for members of the Council for Advancement and Support of Education (CASE). CASE is an association designed to help public information and fundraising professionals in chiefly nonprofit educational institutions. Articles appearing in *Currents* cover topics related to fundraising and public information/relations in this field. Council for Advancement and Support of Education, Suite 400, Eleven Dupont Circle,

Washington, D.C. 20036.

Nonprofit World Report—The bimonthly magazine of the Society for Nonprofit Organizations. Contains articles and tips on everything from fundraising to communications. The Society for Nonprofit Organizations, 9 Odana Ct., Madison, WI 53719.

Organizations

The Development Association for Christian Institutions (DACI), 4057 Crown Shore Dr., Dallas, TX 75234.

Evangelical Council for Financial Accountability (ECFA), 1825 Eye St., NW, Suite 400, Washington, D.C. 20006.

72022